D1014224

Reggie McNeal combines southern charm with gospel disruption. Just like the Jesus he follows, McNeal realigns God's people with news of the Kingdom. This means everything gets reordered for the sake of God's determination "to make all things new." McNeal continues to point skillfully and faithfully to God's essentials and priorities, which recast church and life in Kingdom terms.

DR. MARK LABBERTON
President, Fuller Theological Seminary

In *Kingdom Come*, Reggie McNeal masterfully does what we've come to expect of him: intersecting the path of our past with the reality of the present in order to guide and challenge us toward a new and better direction for the future. Why listen to him? He looks out the window, sees what most of us are too busy to see, and challenges us to new thinking.

TODD WILSON
Cofounder and director, Exponential

Reggie McNeal has written an exuberant, humble, clear, timely, nearly unassailable call-to-arms for Jesus followers to radically shift their focus from Churchianity to the Kingdom of God—*life as God intends it*. We must rediscover our essential task as partners in God's redemptive mission for the world, or lose our claim to relevance in a culture that is quickly abandoning propositional Christianity that has been hermetically sealed in competitive silos of shrinking market share. Breaking free from brittle, self-imposed constraints, Reggie calls us to join hands and hearts in the common purpose of loving God by loving our neighbors in as many life-honoring ways as health and wholeness reveal.

THE REV. DR. STEPHEN BAUMAN
Christ Church, United Methodist, New York City

Kudos to Reggie McNeal, who is out to return us from Churchianity to Christianity. Read this book to understand that the church is not a club, but a launching pad; that discipleship's about a direction (following Jesus), not a doctrine; and that the gospel story's star is God, not your church. May *Kingdom Come* help us recalibrate so that we may live out the Abrahamic call to bless our cities and the nations.

DR. AMY L. SHERMAN
Author of *Kingdom Calling*

I appreciated reading Reggie McNeal's *Kingdom Come*. As usual with this author, I felt alternately affirmed, challenged, and occasionally bothered by his candid insights on the church and contemporary culture. It reads like a manifesto for mission, calling for Christian leaders to seriously consider the true Kingdom impact their ministry is having on the community they are called to serve.

BARRY SWANSON
Commissioner of the Eastern Territory, Salvation Army USA

Reggie gives us a compelling thesis on unlocking the congregation's social power from within today's churches. He offers a blueprint for building greater Kingdom communities, where congregations find spiritual fulfillment in Kingdom service. Imagine the strength of church foundations built on the rocks of its people's collaborative spirit and on mission work with and for the community. The Kingdom can come, and never has the need been greater.

SAM OLIVER
Global supply chain production lead, Monsanto

Are we, as the church, supposed to get our hands dirty in the pressing issues of our communities? If the Kingdom is essentially "life as God intends for it to be," as Reggie McNeal contends so convincingly in this book, and if we see that our community is not as God intends, then we have our answer. In that light, the church is no longer the end; it is the means.

JIM MORGAN
President, Meet the Need

Our missional coach is back to his meddling business. Reggie makes a biblical case that if congregations are going to be involved in what God is up to, they must move from their predictable church ministry focus to a Kingdom mission focus. Churches may be dying, but God's Kingdom is thriving. This book has the potential, with the Spirit's help, to wake us up from "missional amnesia" and launch us into vital, life-giving mission.

DR. MARNIE CRUMPLER
Executive pastor, Peachtree Presbyterian Church

Kingdom Come can transform our country's education system! Reggie McNeal inspires Kingdom growth in our schools and communities with examples of people who are partnering with God and their local schools. Classroom teachers alone cannot meet the educational, health, and social needs of all children. It takes a Kingdom approach. Practical and stirring advice on how to be *on mission* with God with issues that stir your heart.

MELANIE BARTON
Executive director, South Carolina Education Oversight Committee

One of the first songs my children learned was "Seek Ye First the Kingdom of God." I admit I never was sure exactly what that meant until now. Open this book, underline every word, and as God's people, partner with Him in helping people live a better life—abundant life! May His Kingdom come!

JUDY LEE
Executive director, Titus County Cares

KINGDOM
COME

KINGDOM COME

*Why We Must Give Up Our Obsession with Fixing
the Church—and What We Should Do Instead*

REGGIE MCNEAL

**TYNDALE®
MOMENTUM**

*An Imprint of
Tyndale House Publishers, Inc.*

Visit Tyndale online at www.tyndale.com.

Visit Tyndale Momentum online at www.tyndalemomentum.com.

TYNDALE, *Tyndale Momentum,* and the Tyndale Momentum logo are registered trademarks of Tyndale House Publishers, Inc. Tyndale Momentum is an imprint of Tyndale House Publishers, Inc., Carol Stream, Illinois.

Kingdom Come: Why We Must Give Up Our Obsession with Fixing the Church—and What We Should Do Instead

Copyright © 2015 by Reggie McNeal. All rights reserved.

Cover photograph copyright © Lonely/DollarPhotoClub. All rights reserved.

Designed by Stephen Vosloo

Published in association with the literary agency of Mark Sweeney and Associates, Bonita Springs, Florida 34135.

Unless otherwise indicated, all Scripture quotations are taken from the *Holy Bible,* New Living Translation, copyright © 1996, 2004, 2007, 2013 by Tyndale House Foundation. Used by permission of Tyndale House Publishers, Inc., Carol Stream, Illinois 60188. All rights reserved.

Scripture quotations marked NIV are taken from the Holy Bible, *New International Version,*® *NIV.*® Copyright © 1973, 1978, 1984, 2011 by Biblica, Inc.® Used by permission. All rights reserved worldwide.

Library of Congress Cataloging-in-Publication Data

McNeal, Reggie.
   Kingdom come : Why we must give up our obsession with fixing the church, and what we should do instead / Reggie McNeal.
     pages cm
   Includes bibliographical references.
    ISBN 978-1-4143-9187-8 (sc)
1. Kingdom of God. 2. Mission of the church. 3. Eschatology. I. Title.
   BT94.M365 2015
   231.7'2—dc23   2015000630

Printed in the United States of America

21	20	19	18	17	16
7	6	5	4	3	2

CONTENTS

Introduction *xi*

1 My Journey into the Kingdom *1*

2 Kingdom Tales *19*

3 The Heroic Kingdom Narrative *39*

4 Challenging the Church's Storyline *59*

5 Aiding and Abetting the Kingdom *85*

6 When It Works: Kingdom Collaboration *109*

7 Making the Move *133*

8 What Now? *161*

Conclusion *177*

Notes *181*

Discussion Questions *183*

About the Author *193*

Also by Reggie McNeal *195*

INTRODUCTION

I WAS THE GUEST SPEAKER AT a Lutheran church on Reformation Sunday, a high holy day for this denominational tribe that feels a special connection to the Reformation. This particular congregation had pulled out all the stops—literally. Their pipe organ was at full throttle. The choirs sang, the handbell ringers rang, the orchestra swelled, and all the banners were unfurled. It was great pageantry, and I loved every minute of it.

My assignment that morning was to challenge the church to move forward into the future. After acknowledging the historical significance of Martin Luther in the progression of Christianity, I turned my comments to the church's next chapter.

"We've been working at 'fixing' the church for the past five hundred years," I said. "How's that going for us?"

I reflected on the fact that, in my lifetime alone, we've been through the personal evangelism movement, the church renewal movement, the church growth movement, the worship wars, the church health craze, and the charismatic and neo-charismatic doctrinal debates (just to name a few of the topics that have captured the attention of church leaders). After sharing some current statistics about the growing disaffection of Americans with institutional religion, I proposed an alternative approach: "Why not just do what the church *should* be doing—partnering with God in his redemptive mission in the world—and let the overflow of that effort bring about the renewal we're looking for?"

Put another way, it's time for a change in the narrative we're using to express the identity and mission of the church. Obsessing over "fixing the church" has created a church-centered storyline that not only misses the point but also often runs counter to the narrative that God intends for us to live into and out of—namely, the saga of the Kingdom of God. It's time for the church to get over its self-absorption and self-centeredness and adopt the larger and more compelling story of God's Kingdom as its reason for being and its mission in the world.

The problem is that we don't see the problem with these competing narratives. That's because too many church people confuse the two storylines. From what I've observed, most Christians seem to believe that the *church* and the *Kingdom* of God are one and the same—that is, if they've even studied or been taught about the Kingdom (which I know from my own experience growing up is not a given).

In any case, there's a widely held set of beliefs among churchgoers that (1) God's primary agenda on earth focuses on building the church; (2) what happens on Sunday mornings largely defines the mission and ministry of the church; and (3) if people aren't going to church on Sunday, then something is terribly messed up with the pursuit of God's agenda.

In the context of these beliefs, the growing cultural disaffection with the institutional church is a pretty discouraging situation. A 2012 Pew Study of Religion in America showed that one in five Americans now claim "nonaffiliated" as their religious identification—up from one in six in 2007. For the Millennial generation, that number is almost one in three (32 percent)—up from one in four just five years earlier!

Certainly, if we believe that the church as a cultural institution is at the center of God's work in the world, it's an alarming trend. But if we recognize that it is actually the Kingdom of Heaven that is at the center of God's plan and purpose, well, the church occupies a much stronger position.

Potentially.

If we get our story straight.

A better future for the church requires that we realign our theology and practice with the primary storyline of the Kingdom.

Let's see if we can untangle the competing storylines.

The word *church* appears only three times in most modern English translations of the Gospels (once in Matthew 16:18 and twice in Matthew 18:17). In each instance, the underlying Greek word is *ekklesia*, which was a familiar word in the first century that referred not to a place or a program but to an *assembly of people*. Specifically, these were people "called out" from among the community to serve the town or village by looking after its welfare—a kind of eldership. This word that connotes "a stewardship of community life" is the one that Jesus chose to designate his followers. By definition, the church (*ekklesia*) was never supposed to focus on itself. The interests and issues of the *community* were the rightful scope of its agenda.

In comparison, the Gospels contain thirty-one references to the Kingdom of Heaven (all in Matthew) and fifty-one mentions of the Kingdom of God (throughout all four Gospels). In teaching his disciples, Jesus focused far more on the *Kingdom* than on the *assembly*.

Surely this emphasis gives us a clue about what captures the heart of God. Jesus also talked a lot about how we treat one another, especially when it comes to the poor and disadvantaged. He called us to a life of meeting the needs of others and alleviating the suffering and pain that is naturally part of living in a broken world.

To drive home his point, Jesus healed people of disease, dysfunction, and disfigurement to show us the Kingdom in action and to demonstrate God's intention to redeem human existence in every dimension—physical, emotional, and spiritual. And when he taught his followers to pray, he made it clear that the priority of the Kingdom of Heaven is to manifest itself on earth—not just by and by, but here and now! In other words, Jesus wants us to pray for, deeply desire, and dedicate ourselves to seeing the Kingdom as it operates in heaven made *visible* and *active* in our daily experience here on earth.

Still, it has been difficult for many churchgoers in our society to get a handle on the Kingdom. Our classic definitions, such as "the rule and reign of God," make it seem a distant and fuzzy reality. We know that Jesus taught his disciples to pray that God's Kingdom would come and that his will would be done "on earth as it is in heaven," but we've had trouble translating these concepts into real-time, real-life applications.

The Kingdom champions the life that God intends for all of us to experience on *this* planet, in *this* lifetime. This epic adventure is worthy of our lives because it is the story of life as God has always intended—where good triumphs over evil and light chases away darkness. God's perfect plan will not be fully realized until Jesus returns, but in the meantime he wants us to pray that the Kingdom will break *in* to our hearts, bringing transformation to our lives, and break *out* into the world, bringing hope amid hurt and fostering a better world in the face of immense problems, as we refuse to allow evil and suffering to have the final word in our lives. Talk about a compelling story!

At the end of a lengthy teaching about the Kingdom of Heaven in Matthew 13, Jesus says to his disciples, "Every teacher of the law *who has become a disciple in the kingdom of heaven* is like the owner of a house who brings out of his storeroom new treasures as well as old" (Matthew 13:52, NIV, emphasis added). Whatever else we might glean from this verse, I believe two points are clear:

1. Jesus draws a distinction between teachers who have become disciples in the Kingdom of Heaven and ones who have not.

2. Those teachers who have become disciples in the Kingdom of Heaven don't abandon the "old" treasures, but they bring out "new treasures as well."

OK, I'm intrigued

My desire in these pages is to unpack some of the treasures that have been hidden or buried and whose time to be "brought out of the storeroom" is long overdue. As we'll see, they've been hiding in plain sight all along.

I believe that God is looking for pastors, leaders, and individual Jesus-followers who are willing to become disciples in the Kingdom of Heaven and thereby further the Kingdom agenda here on earth. The Kingdom has always been operating, but the question is whether we in the church will align ourselves with Kingdom priorities and Kingdom purposes and allow the Kingdom to focus and guide our lives.

The key to unleashing the promise of the Kingdom does not lie in our figuring out how to "do church better." We have great bands, laser light shows, amazing health clubs, incredible worship extravaganzas, engaging sermons, and good coffee—finally! In other words, we do church fabulously well. Obsessing over this issue is an unworthy and unbiblical, even idolatrous, pursuit. Instead, the church must embrace and embody a new narrative driven by Kingdom concerns instead of church issues.

Background Information

Before we can change our cultural narrative for the better, the church must change its own internal narrative. For starters, we must recognize that the church and the Kingdom are not one and the same. We must draw some key distinctions if we want to see things in their proper perspective. Here are just a few examples to show you what I mean:

1. The church's role as a vital force in society is increasingly in question. The Kingdom of Heaven, on the other hand, is never irrelevant. God's plan and purpose in the world are always cutting edge because the Kingdom is all about bringing healing to the afflicted, binding up the brokenhearted, releasing people from captivity, and redeeming everything diminished by sin.

   If church leaders would unbundle the social capital in their organizations to join God in his Kingdom work, many communities across North America would experience a significant improvement in the quality of people's lives. Aligning the church with the Kingdom will both serve the community and save the church from missional irrelevance.

2. The church, as commonly configured, is often centered on activities among church people on church property for church purposes, and can become focused on preserving and perpetuating the program. In contrast, the Kingdom of Heaven is an *invading force*, expanding the rule and reign of God against a dark kingdom that will inevitably collapse. God invites us to participate in his liberation campaign, but the Kingdom moves forward whether we choose to participate or not. If we opt out, we will miss the abundant life that God has in mind for us. But if we respond to Jesus' call to live as Kingdom agents *everywhere we go*, we will experience the joy of seeing God at work. Once

you've witnessed a few resurrections, everything else pales in comparison!

3. The current scorecard by which many churches in North America measure their progress and success does not adequately reflect Kingdom values or the Kingdom agenda. What is considered important (as seen by what they measure) often reinforces a narrative at odds with the Kingdom of God.

     Millions of well-meaning Jesus-followers have been led to believe that their primary spiritual identity is their church affiliation and that their devotion to God is measured by church-centered metrics such as participation in, and support of, church activities.

     If these efforts contributed to the advance of the Kingdom, that would be one thing. But the sad truth is that much of the activity in the church actually *hinders* Kingdom expression by gobbling up time, talent, and treasure to support, maintain, and perpetuate church programs.

4. In a Kingdom-centered understanding of the church, the gathering of like-minded believers doesn't go away. In fact, it becomes even more essential for worship, encouragement, instruction, and fellowship. But those activities won't be seen as ends in themselves, and success will not be defined by the size of the gathering, the sublimity of the sermon, or the "sense of God's presence" on a given Sunday. The church is not the point of the Kingdom; the Kingdom is the point of the church. Jesus taught us to pray "thy Kingdom

Litsch's but true

come," not "thy church come." The church is a subset of Kingdom activity. The Kingdom is not a subset of church activity. The Kingdom has a much more expansive mission than can be expressed through the institutional church. The Kingdom agenda involves every single aspect of God's work in the world. By definition, most of what God does happens outside the church. The church has a vital role to play, but the church is not the center of the action.

5. Too often, the church has made "being saved" the point. Certainly, we have been saved from the penalty of sin through the work of Jesus Christ on the cross, but the story doesn't end there. We've not only been saved *from* something; we've also been saved *for* something, and that something is the work of the Kingdom. When we discover this and give our lives to it, we'll begin to see the full story unfold.

6. The church is not eternal, but the Kingdom of God is. God's purpose and plan predate the church and will play out beyond the reaches of human history. God's mission was already underway in the Garden of Eden, and it will reach its fulfillment after the church has accomplished its work and has been folded into the eternal Kingdom.

Can We Talk?

From the responses I've received to a few of my previous books, I know some people think that I believe the institutional church has little role in the Kingdom and that

I'm allergic to any kind of organized religious expression. Nothing could be further from the truth. Both my theology and my personal practice involve the assembling of the body of Christ. Let me be clear: There is no such thing as privatized spirituality for Jesus-followers. After all, we have Trinitarian DNA in our blood!

Others have suggested that my observations—and, yes, my critiques of current church practice—merely serve up more deconstructive criticism. That's why I have gone to great lengths in this book to build my case from scriptural and theological foundations, as well as to offer alternative behaviors and practices in the hope of moving the discussion forward. In other words, I'm not interested in tearing down the church. I want to help it genuinely flourish by regaining its proper identity and role. Wherever we may disagree in the pages to follow, I hope we can be of one mind on this central idea: *The purpose of the church is to further God's Kingdom.* If we can agree on that, I believe we can find enough room to come together and talk.

Speaking to pastors and other church leaders in particular, I hope you will feel challenged, not attacked; inspired, not besieged; and supported, not undermined. As teachers and shepherds, you have an indispensable role to play in the Kingdom narrative. My hope is that, as a result of your courageous leadership, a Kingdom-centered agenda will begin to crowd out church-centered activity—not to push the church to the margins but to nudge it toward its proper place in the Kingdom.

We can be encouraged by the good news that the Kingdom of Heaven is doing just fine. It is ever-present, ever-working, and ever-expanding. When I said this recently to a group of about five dozen pastors, they looked confused, as if it had never occurred to them that the Kingdom of God is not at risk. I told them all to relax, that God is quite capable of managing his own Kingdom and doesn't need our help to get his work done or to advance his position (which isn't to say that he does not make use of us in these ways).

My urgency in writing and speaking on this topic is not rooted in the fear that the Kingdom will suffer unless we somehow "get it" and do it right. My urgency is rooted in the desire that we *not miss out* on being a part of what God is *already* doing in the world. My hope is that the church will change its story and align with God's mission, and that we'll begin to see the Kingdom breaking out all over.

Many church leaders and Jesus-followers already get this message and are working like crazy to share and embody the Kingdom story. I work with a growing cadre of Kingdom agents—individual Jesus-followers, leaders of congregations and church networks, and teams of cross-domain community members and leaders. Some of them have been at it for years. Some are just getting their feet wet. They all are doing incredible work to move the needle on big societal issues—Kingdom issues—from tackling poverty to improving education, from expanding health-care access to fostering economic development. If it involves raising the quality of life (an important aspect of the "abundant life" that Jesus spoke of) for people made in the image of God, they are all in.

Consider this book your invitation to *get in the game* if you're not already, or an encouragement to *press on* if the Kingdom has already become your primary work and focus.

These are good things, but I might need convincing that they are Kingdom issues

Jesus has always had plans for the church. He still does. But his plans do not center on the church. His designs for us involve a much bigger story, maybe a different one than what you've heard about at church on Sunday.

That was certainly true for me.

MY JOURNEY INTO THE KINGDOM

I WAS A CHURCH PERSON before I was even born, attending services in my mother's womb for nine months before showing up to claim my spot in the church nursery. My dad was a Southern Baptist pastor, and my early spiritual life revolved around the church. I made my profession of faith when I was nine years old, walking the aisle during the hymn of invitation to publicly declare that Jesus was my Savior and Lord. By that same action, I also joined the church as a member, and I was baptized some weeks later as the culmination of that process. My baptism was celebrated as a church ordinance, took place in a church sanctuary, and was witnessed by a roomful of church people. It was a full-on church experience, signifying that I was now officially one of them.

The Kingdom of God was never mentioned during this pivotal time in my life. I didn't have the foggiest notion about the Kingdom or what part it played in my connection with God. For me, and for everyone I knew, it was all about the church. We demonstrated our Christian commitment by being good church members.

At some point, news of the Kingdom of God penetrated my consciousness, but it was viewed through the lens of church culture, leading (I now see) to a skewed understanding of the Kingdom and its place in God's plan for the world. The Kingdom was seen as a subset of church activity—more of a catchphrase to describe extraordinary church activities—rather than the main purpose for God's work in the world. So, for example, if two congregations came together to do some church thing—such as a youth fellowship event after a football game—that cooperative effort was called a Kingdom endeavor. The Kingdom was like the church on steroids—at least, that's how I understood it.

Later, as my denomination got caught up in the culture wars undertaken by conservative evangelical church leaders, the Kingdom designation was extended to include efforts by which the church sought to influence the political arena. Thus, crusades against various evils, certain leaders, and high-profile Supreme Court decisions were deemed Kingdom engagements. The clear belief was that the Kingdom of God was under assault and that it was up to us in the church to protect it and save it.

Because the church and the Kingdom were synonymous according to this paradigm, anything that threatened the church or diminished the role of the church in society was seen as a direct assault on the Kingdom. We didn't have to look very far to find evidence of Kingdom erosion. Blue laws were collapsing, church attendance was waning, and countless other distractions were tearing at Christendom's hold on the culture.

Unfortunately, the church's budding siege mentality served to further its inward-turning self-absorption. The church-growth movement among evangelical Protestants and the Second Vatican Council in the Catholic Church were touted as efforts to connect with contemporary culture. But in reality those initiatives were driven by institutional concerns for survival. The rise of megachurches in the latter decades of the twentieth century—and the sense of growth and progress generated by shifting church attendance from the "mom and pop" churches to the "superstores"—masked the decline of Christendom and the church's influence in the culture.

Because *church* and *Kingdom* were seen as interchangeable terms for the same spiritual reality, things weren't looking too good for the home team. And, in fact, that "home team" mentality was part of the problem. We thought of ourselves as playing out the Kingdom game on our home turf, the church. As Sunday went, so went the Kingdom. Our church-centered scorecards celebrated church activities on church property led by church people for other church people. Everything else—vocations, hobbies, the rest of life outside the church—wasn't Kingdom related. Simply put, if it didn't show up at church, it didn't count. The perceived line between what was spiritual and what was merely secular was firmly drawn.

An old and familiar concept!

I began my preparation to go into ministry just as the church-growth movement was taking off and the seeker-friendly model was being formulated. The evolving conversation about ways to "reach the lost world" at least acknowledged that a world requiring some intentional engagement existed "out there." But my thinking, along with that of most other church leaders at the time, was still very much centered on the church and its activities. The work of God in the world was anchored in the church and played out in the church. The aim was to get people into church, where God could somehow get ahold of them. And the church would grow if it was doing the right things.

Then, late in my seminary sojourn, I read some books that really messed up my view of the church. Beginning with Howard Snyder's *The Problem of Wineskins* and *The Community of the King*, I came face-to-face with a radical, new (to me) idea—namely, that the key to church renewal lies in anchoring the mission and purpose of the church in the biblical teaching of what it means to be the people of God.

These books were the first I had encountered that highlighted the discussion of the church's mission in the world. (Most books I was reading at the time dealt with some aspect of "doing church better"—improving existing practices without asking questions about why we were doing things the way we were or whether we should be doing them in the first place.) Snyder's observations and critiques unsettled me, especially when he pointed out how much Jesus struggled with the religious institutions of *his* day.

I had grown up with a Jesus who loved the church, every single part of it, from the organ prelude to the Vacation

Bible School pledges of allegiance to the American flag, the Christian flag, and the Bible. (I can still recite them all.) The idea that Jesus might not be thrilled with church as I knew it was a stunning revelation and a real wake-up call.

Snyder's books were game changers, beginning a process that has now continued for more than three decades. The journey has involved moving from a church-centered universe to a Kingdom-centered framework, and it has shifted the center of gravity for how I see the world, how I view the work of God in the world, and how I relate to both.

Other writers soon chimed in on the conversation. Some were contemporary; others were ancient. I had done my doctoral work in historical theology, so I began to explore primary sources: the ante-Nicene church fathers, the sixteenth-century Reformers, and leaders of church renewal efforts throughout Christian history. These writers and their ideas expanded my understanding of how the church should express itself. I confess that my ideas were still church-centered rather than Kingdom-centered. I thought if we could just *fix* the church, the Kingdom of God would naturally be released. But I still thought our expression of the Kingdom would primarily be demonstrated through the congregational life and programs of the local church.

As a young church planter after seminary, I was determined to "do church differently," so that it would be more of what God had in mind. However, I still reduced the scope and reach of the Kingdom down to church size as I plotted our congregationally focused ministry. I was convinced that building a great church was our contribution to God's Kingdom. We offered lots of innovative programming—and we did it well—but it was all tethered to the church's facilities. Church people planned, produced, and promoted our activities and programs, which were geared primarily for other church people to consume.

And then it was all taken away. After twenty years of local congregational ministry, I shifted venues to take on a role as a denominational executive and leadership coach. It proved a very challenging transition for my family and me. I loved the part about working with church leaders in their personal development; but I despised the denominational politics, and I couldn't figure out why God would reassign me to something so unappealing. The only clue I had about the repositioning came through something I sensed God saying to me during a personal prayer retreat: *There's someplace you can't get to from where you are.*

For a long time, that was all I had to go on, but now I think I understand. There was a *universe* I couldn't get to from where I was.

A Missional World Dawns

I vividly remember the moment when the shift began. It was like the crackling of ice on a pond in the springtime, which signaled the eventual collapse of the theological and philosophical platform that had supported my entire ministry to that point.

After speaking one day about the future of the church to a group of church leaders in another part of the state, I got in my car and drove home. Late that night, I pulled into the parking lot of the apartment complex where my family and I lived during the transition to my new job. I shut off the engine and began contemplating the thirty-two-step climb to my third-floor apartment.

In the next few moments, before I even got out of the car, I had an unexpected but life-altering thought. It was more of a confession than an insight: *I just spent the past ten years of my life building the perfect church . . . and not a single person in this apartment complex would walk across the street to attend it.*

It was the truth! I had noticed that my family and I were the only ones leaving our apartment community on Sunday morning all dressed up and headed to church. Everyone else was sleeping in, enjoying the pool, or heading to the lake or the mall, and church was nowhere on their list of possible things to do.

What's wrong with this picture? If the church represents the manifest presence of God in the world—the very body of Christ—why was the culture losing interest in it, and why was so much church activity resulting in so little impact?

I spent the better part of the next decade working on this puzzle.

Over time, I came to believe that the church, particularly in North America, suffers from missional amnesia. When the church decided that the mission was about growing the church, doing church better, or even fixing the church, it went off mission, and became misguided, even idolatrous.

The answers I formulated led me to become a champion of the Kingdom and to try to shape the conversation around *missional church*—a term that should be redundant, but unfortunately is not.

The right answer to the question, *What constitutes the mission of the church?* has to do with partnering with God as *his* people in *his* mission. That mission is the Kingdom of God, not the church.

Jesus told us to pray, "Thy Kingdom come," not "Thy church come." Though the church plays a vital role in the Kingdom, it is not the *point* of the Kingdom.

The purpose, goal, and result of the Kingdom is *life*, not church-centered metrics and outcomes. Jesus said, "I have come to give you abundant *life*," not abundant *church*. Moreover, the church is not forever; the Kingdom is.

Those of us in the missional church conversation have made the case for a very different understanding of the church. This perspective (a more biblical perspective, we believe) offers a corrective to the consumerist, preoccupied, and self-absorbed expressions of church that, among other consequences, have given the church a well-deserved poor reputation among many people in our society. The missional understanding of church opens the door to a reevaluation of the relationship between the church and the Kingdom, with an expanded view of God's work in the world.

For missional thinkers, church is a *verb*, a *way of being* in the world. It is not a place where certain religious rites are conducted. Nor is the church a vendor of religious goods and services.[1] The notion of the church as a place, or as a dispenser of programs, is a relic of an era of Christendom that is rapidly diminishing, if not already disappearing beyond the horizon.

In its essence, church is organic, not organizational, though it has institutional and corporate expressions. Church is not a time, a place, or a set of prescribed activities. In short, church is not a *thing*; it's a *who*. It is the people of God.

Everywhere we go, and everything we do, is informed by our relationship with God, just as everything I do (and some things I *don't* do) as a husband are informed by my marriage to my wife. I don't go to my house to be married. I carry my marriage with me everywhere I go.

Likewise, wherever we go, as Jesus-followers in covenant with God, we are (part of) the church. We gather with other believers, worship God, and practice certain spiritual disciplines. But we don't have to "go to church" in order to be "part of" the church because we *are* the church. We're not *all* of the church, but everywhere we go, the church *is*.

Being church is more than just a catchy way of saying it. It means finding organic ways to express our covenantal relationship with God. Church is incarnated in every aspect of our lives, not just as part of our "church experience" in a local congregation. It means that we see all of life as a mission trip.

Missional church seeks to live out our covenantal relationship with God by finding ways to bless people, both corporately (as groups of believers) and individually. Love of God and love of neighbor are inextricably intertwined in a missional understanding of church. Service to others is a fundamental spiritual discipline. And most important, when we are faithful at *being church*, we point people to the Kingdom.

This understanding of church as a mission-centered relationship presents a challenge for those giving leadership to the institutional church. My role for years now has been to help articulate for church leaders the changes that must be made in order to realign the institutional church with its mission, and to help these leaders develop and implement strategies to move in a missional direction. To support these shifts, leaders must make some intentional choices. As I make suggestions and share with you the conclusions I've drawn, you will see how my thinking and experience have led me to a broader view of what God is up to in the world. His agenda is far bigger than building the church. He is building his Kingdom.

Kingdom Insights

Helping congregations and leaders become engaged with their local communities has opened their eyes to a very accessible and ripe "mission field." Many congregations have sent hundreds or thousands of people and millions of dollars around the world to support missions activities, but at the same time they have failed to connect with the school across the street or the apartment complex next door. As soon as congregations truly grasp their mission to partner with God in his redemptive mission in the world, it's only natural that they would begin to engage with their local community. I've seen congregations that, once the blinders were off, were stunned by the depth of need in their very own neighborhood: a world of need that has little to do with church programming but everything to do with real-life issues.

This new awareness of what is happening just outside their doors has provoked a crisis for these leaders and their congregations. But it's a good crisis. When church people confront the reality that much of what they have focused on as a congregation is irrelevant and unhelpful to the very people they are called to serve, they often suddenly find themselves eager to engage in what they have previously thought of as nonchurch activity: tutoring school kids so they can learn to read; teaching English to immigrants so they can assimilate into society; rescuing vulnerable people from human trafficking; and securing affordable housing for families, just to name a few.

Because the Kingdom is about life—*abundant* life, to quote Jesus—I came to realize that all of these life issues are Kingdom concerns. In Jesus' day, a Kingdom outbreak meant that the lame could walk, the blind could see, and the lepers were made whole. Because these physical conditions prevented people from working to support themselves, their disabilities doomed them to beggary and poverty. Delivering people from these maladies made a much better life possible for them.

In our day, manifestations of the Kingdom may still include physical healing, but they also mean that people are freed from limiting conditions that keep them locked into perpetually poor life situations. Thus, Kingdom efforts result in kids learning to read so they have a chance at graduation; the unemployed finding jobs; the uninsured gaining access to adequate health care; and the homeless finding a place to call home.

The Kingdom gives life—not just for those who are served but also for those who serve. Getting in on what God is already up to brings profound, life-giving renewal to congregations and leaders who are taking this path. Many leaders who have become weary of doing church work suddenly find themselves reenergized as they shift their attention and their efforts. Though I still run into clergy every week who are burned out and ready to quit church work, I don't know of a single missional church leader who is ready to throw in the towel. Tired? Yes. Burned out? No! As one leader nearing retirement age recently told me, "I wish I had thirty more years for ministry." This desire stands in stark contrast to the sentiment he expressed in our first conversation several years ago, when he complained to me that he was bored and "barely hanging on." What brought about this change in perspective, energy, and drive? He shifted his ministry focus from church programming to community development. Specifically, he led his congregation in developing a citywide network of after-school resource centers to bring help and hope to kids who are locked up in generational and institutional poverty.

Kingdom engagement thrusts us into situations where abundant life is threatened, compromised, or missing, so that we can serve as advocates for the life that God intends for people to experience. Kingdom enterprise completes the storyline of salvation that all too often has been truncated in our understanding and presentation of the gospel. We assert that we've been saved *from* a previous existence *through* the work of Jesus on the cross. And that's all true. But there's more to it than that. We've also been saved *to* something— namely, eternal life in the Kingdom. Kingdom life is a life of good deeds and service to others. It's worth doing. In giving away our lives, we gain them back. We ourselves pass from death to life as we help others do the same.

I believe that many Jesus-followers are intimidated by the idea of Kingdom life because we've misperceived, or been misinformed about, what it requires. We tend to think of Kingdom living as something extreme or bizarre. This view has been fueled by a recent spate of books in Christian circles suggesting that disciples of Jesus should live dramatically different lives in order to reflect countercultural Kingdom values. These authors are right, of course, and what I'm about to say is not intended as criticism of their work. (After all, sometimes you have to shout just to get people's attention, so I understand what they are doing.)

Unfortunately, what most often sticks in people's minds are the examples of the more radical, disruptive lifestyle choices. Most people can't give away everything they have, so they draw the wrong conclusion that they cannot be Kingdom-centered in their faith. This is not what these books advocate, by the way, but the enemy whose kingdom we are invading blows things out of proportion to scare us off from considering how we can amend our lives for greater Kingdom impact.

Jesus certainly calls us to a radically different way of life in the Kingdom. It is a call to be people of blessing; to live lives of generosity and grace, service and sensitivity; to be positive examples of joy and contentment in a culture awash in negativity and anxiety. One can hardly be more counter-cultural than to believe one can make a difference in our communities and then to act on that belief. Throughout this book, I cite examples of everyday people, in their ordinary circumstances, pushing back the darkness where they live, work, play, and go to school.

What is true for us as individuals also holds true for our corporate expressions as the people of God. If you're a church leader, you might be tempted to think that only organic and emerging-church life-forms (such as missional communities) can adopt a Kingdom-centered ministry. Don't fall into that trap. A house church can be incredibly self-absorbed while a large congregation can pursue an agenda aimed at releasing its social capital to bless its community in profound ways. No matter what form of church expression you currently serve as a leader or a congregant, you can move it toward greater Kingdom-centeredness.

Bottom line: I wrote this book for the vast majority of pastors, leaders, and individual Jesus-followers who want to explore and experience the Kingdom in the places in which they are assigned and in ways that are winsome, doable, and sustainable. As citizens of God's Kingdom, we want to live our everyday lives, in all our life arenas, as people of blessing who help other people experience life as God intends.

As congregations I've consulted with have adopted schools, partnered with local food banks, and worked with neighborhood organizations in various projects, they (and I) have discovered that these issues are too big for any one person to accomplish alone. "We need each other" is a fundamental principle of the Kingdom.

This interdependence is a good thing because it leads us to another discovery: God already has people at work in these vineyards. Often they are people of faith who have been quietly engaged in the business of helping others. A friend of mine who works with an urban ministry in a major city told me about a time when he ran into one of his homeless clients at a nursing home. When asked why he was there, the homeless man said, "I just come here to visit people who don't have anybody to visit them." The staff at the facility confirmed that the homeless man had been doing this for years.

When God's people come out to play—when we decide to move out of the cloister of the church and into the neighborhoods and the streets, where people are—we find we have lots of company. Just as God has not restricted his Kingdom activity to the church domain, he is not restricted in whom he uses in his Kingdom endeavors. The Scriptures testify to times when he used even wicked kings and rulers (Cyrus of Persia, Herod the Great, and Nero, to name a few) to accomplish his Kingdom purposes. He also uses ordinary people, many of whom are not church people. God has his Kingdom agents everywhere, battling society's ills in every community, even when they don't know they are his Kingdom agents. How much more would he do if we were to unbundle the pent-up social and financial capital of the people inside the walls of so many church buildings?

Moving Ahead

From what I've seen, the church in America abandoned the culture long before the culture abandoned the church. A century ago, the church built hospitals, schools, and nursing homes and operated soup kitchens, orphanages, and community shelters. The people of God were heavily invested in meeting basic human and social needs. Unfortunately, the rise of the fundamentalist movement in the early twentieth century introduced forces that radically altered the church's engagement with the culture. In reaction to the often harsh dogmatism of the fundamentalists, mainline denominations dropped the spiritual emphasis in their social ministries, though they stayed socially engaged. The new evangelicals who emerged, on the other hand, retreated from the social arena to build great congregations, believing this to be the way to help people navigate the fallen world. Both approaches failed society, falling short of the biblical admonition to speak the truth in love (Ephesians 4:15). The mainliners loved people without telling them the whole truth spiritually. The evangelicals told the truth, but often in ways that came across as unloving.

Truth linked with love, taught, and demonstrated—this was the way of Jesus. This path provides the only authentic way forward for the church to regain its credibility, by reshaping its narrative to match the Kingdom storyline.

Over the past two decades, I have been encouraged as I've seen the missional-church movement gain traction. As it has, I've seen the scope of the church's engagement with the local community accelerate. In the early days, I was thrilled if a congregation would set aside one day a year to go out and serve the community somehow. Lately, I've worked with clients who have secured some epic wins, such as raising a quarter-million pounds of food in one week for their region's food bank, eliminating childhood illiteracy in their community, reducing the number of hungry kids in their school district to zero, or establishing a community-based case-worker system to take care of at-risk populations.

As recently as a decade ago, my work was primarily with church teams who often struggled to name two or three city leaders with whom they had any level of relationship. Now I work with city leaders across all domains and sectors of society, many of whom are people of faith, who possess enormous personal passion to leverage their significant positions of influence in order to have a positive impact on their cities. They are eager to partner with faith organizations to work for the common good. Rather than demonstrating allergic reactions to working with church leaders, they are beseeching and recruiting church leaders to join them. Though they're not waiting around for the church before pursuing their convictions, they welcome the arrival of churches that are willing to invest in community development and bless the city. This is good news for the church. It is the gospel of the Kingdom coming to fruition.

It's time for the people of God to throw a party. A street party. A Kingdom party. A party for life, here and now, on earth as it is in heaven. A renewed focus on the Kingdom here and now promises help and hope for our communities. It may also halt the church's slide into irrelevance in the eyes of the wider culture.

But let's not get ahead of ourselves. All this talk of the Kingdom raises an obvious question: "What is the Kingdom, anyway?"

I'm glad you asked.

KINGDOM TALES

THE CONCEPT OF KINGDOMS IS deeply embedded in our collective human narrative. In some measure, the story of civilization, from the dawn of written records down through our present day, is framed and filled by the stories of kingdoms. Even modern republics such as the United States and France have a king or kingdom stories somewhere in their past that contributed to their development.

Many of the stories in the Bible play out against a backdrop of a succession of kingdoms—Egyptian, Canaanite, Assyrian, Babylonian, Persian, Greek, and Roman. Each of these empires rose and fell in turn, following a similar trajectory. Each was led by a succession of kings who conquered and subjugated people groups, administered domestic agendas, and navigated international affairs. The Old Testament history of the people of God is enmeshed in chronicles of these local and regional kingdoms, along with the rise of Israel from its nomadic roots to its establishment as a kingdom of its own. In the New Testament, the storylines of Jesus and the early church take place on a world stage dominated by the Roman Empire.

In our modern popular culture, literature, movies, and video games—such as *The Lord of the Rings*, the Chronicles of Narnia, and *World of Warcraft*—often construct storylines around plots involving kings and kingdoms. Even when we create alien sagas—such as *Star Wars* or *Thor*—we often imagine worlds in which kings and kingdoms play a central role.

Given the prevalence of kingdom stories in human history, we should not be surprised that the idea of a kingdom would serve as a foundational element in the narrative of two interrelated faith expressions. In both Judaism and Christianity, the Kingdom of God plays a dominant role in the story of God's people.

The Kingdom of God, however, remains distinct from any human kingdom in two very important ways.

First, it is a kingdom that does not wax nor wane but is eternal. "Your kingdom is an everlasting kingdom," declares the psalmist (Psalm 145:13). After all, the king of this kingdom never dies.

Second, this kingdom is not terrestrial. In his trial before Pontius Pilate, Jesus stated clearly: "My Kingdom is not an earthly kingdom. . . . My Kingdom is not of this world" (John 18:36).

On the other hand, the Kingdom of God bears striking similarities to human kingdoms in three key ways.

First, even though God's Kingdom has nonterrestrial origins, it manifests itself on earth. Jesus taught his disciples to pray that God's heavenly Kingdom would show itself on earth, reflecting the king's agenda and desires (Matthew 6:10).

Second, like its earthly counterparts, the Kingdom of God reflects the character of the king who sits on the throne. In Psalm 145, David (himself a king) declares that the King-God is worthy of praise for his power, immeasurable greatness, glorious splendor, wonderful miracles, awe-inspiring deeds, wonderful goodness, righteousness, mercy, compassion, slowness to anger, and unfailing love. All this leads David to exclaim, "All of your works will thank you, LORD, and your faithful followers will praise you. They will speak of the glory of your kingdom" (verses 10-11). These attributes are part and parcel of God's Kingdom because of who he is.

A third similarity between the Kingdom of Heaven and the kingdoms of earth centers on the fact that God's Kingdom is engaged in a struggle. Earthly kingdoms have enemies—both from within and without—and all earthly kingdoms eventually succumb to one or more of these foes. The Kingdom of God also finds itself at war, waging a battle against another sinister kingdom on multiple fronts. But here's where the similarities end, because the question of which kingdom will prevail has already been settled. The Kingdom of God is safe and secure—forever. Unlike earthly kingdoms, its future is not in doubt. It triumphs over all its enemies. The story of this conflict—which still rages, though the outcome is certain—is the great chronicle of the Kingdom of God revealed to us, most supremely in Jesus' teaching and life mission.

But even though the Kingdom of Heaven is the archetype for every human kingdom, and even though the Bible offers enormous insight into the workings of this fundamental form of governance, it seems the Kingdom of God suffers neglect in the narrative of the church in the United States. This underappreciation for the centrality of the Kingdom in the overall story of humanity not only has led to a lack of Kingdom-consciousness among church leaders and other Jesus-followers, but has also contributed to a major disconnect between the activity of the church and the life of the Kingdom.

This sad state of affairs is reflected in the development of a competing storyline that has taken center stage in our understanding and experience of what the church (or simply *church*, as a place we attend) is all about. This rival script has become so pervasive that many people don't remember, or have never heard, the Kingdom story. As this replacement narrative has begun to lose its currency in contemporary culture, the influence and efficacy of the church has declined as well, even among Christians. No longer captivated by the church's story, many people are leaving—not because they are losing their faith, but in order to preserve it. Millions more are maintaining their church ties and attendance but are no longer constructively engaged, like the man who said to me recently, "I'm going to church as an example to my grandkids, but I am completely bored with it."

What still gives me hope, however, and what I have seen

as I have traveled the country and met with churches and church leaders, is that these same people are highly susceptible to being captured by the more compelling story of the Kingdom. Every time I talk to church crowds about how they can become more involved in the Kingdom story, it's as if I've announced a jailbreak!

Understanding the Kingdom

So let's define our terms. What is this Kingdom of God (or Kingdom of Heaven, depending on which Gospel you read) and Kingdom narrative I keep talking about?

The Kingdom of God is life as God intends it to be, his original blueprint for all of creation. The Kingdom narrative is the grand and heroic story of what God has done, and will do, to bring about the fulfillment of his plan and purpose for the universe. I offer these statements not so much as definitions, but as characterizations. They cannot begin to encompass the meaning of what they describe. The Kingdom of God and its attending storylines are too big to be reduced to mere definitions. This is why, when Jesus spoke of the Kingdom, he frequently said, "The Kingdom of Heaven is like . . . ," and then he would supply a metaphor or tell a story to illustrate an aspect of the Kingdom.

In suggesting that the Kingdom of God can be characterized as "life as God intends it to be," I imagine the broadest possible application, extending to the entire created order. Humanity is only part of the spectrum of life contained in the Kingdom. The angelic hosts, as well as all the nonhuman organisms that populate the ecosystems on our planet and everywhere else in the universe, constitute part of the

Kingdom. All life and everything that supports life have their origin in God, who alone is the giver of life. There is no other source. Wherever you find life, you find God, for life is his signature, his fingerprint.

Thus, all life endeavors are part of God's Kingdom. This means that the activities of every living thing and being are of central interest to God, from the assignments of the angels in heaven to human stewardship of planet Earth (the first commission given to the primal couple in Eden) to the functions of the tiniest microbes that sustain various ecological and biological systems.

But for our purposes, most of what we need to understand about the Kingdom of God focuses on its implications for our humanity.

In the story of the Garden of Eden, God created everything but human beings by voice command: "And God said, 'Let there be . . .'" But when it came time to create humanity, he got his hands dirty; he became very intimate and personal with his handiwork. After molding Adam "of dust from the ground," God did something extraordinary. He breathed into this new being "the breath of life" (Genesis 2:7). God's first gift to us humans is *life*—straight from himself!

It is because of this auspicious beginning that the scope of human endeavor expresses the depth and breadth of God's Kingdom agenda on earth. Our relationship with God and our human interactions—with ourselves, with one another, with other living beings, and with the planet itself—all fall into the category of the Kingdom. This means that Kingdom concerns extend well beyond what we generally think of as spiritual matters to include culture, art, literature, health, education, politics, business and economics, the environment—the full range of human enterprise and its consequences. If humans are involved in it, the Kingdom of God has a stake in it.

I'm not convinced

That isn't to suggest that human initiatives set the agenda for the Kingdom. It is, after all, the Kingdom of God. It has a King. The King's character and will shape and express the Kingdom's intentions. Practically speaking, this means that, whenever and wherever God's character and will are displayed, the Kingdom is made evident. Goodness is an outcropping of God's Kingdom, as is faithfulness, mercy, compassion, love, justice, righteousness, and sanctity. Whoever is involved in whatever activity that reflects these elements participates in the Kingdom, whether consciously and intentionally or not.

Yeah?

Life as God intends it is *full* life, *abundant* life. Jesus expressed this sentiment when he declared, "My purpose is to give them a rich and satisfying life" (John 10:10). As creatures made in the image of God, we are drawn to this promise because we sense it is the life we were made for. We're attracted to the promise of abundant life because, in the center of our beings, we know there is more to life than what we often experience.

These aspirations we share as human beings are rooted in the grand narrative of the Kingdom.

Eden and the Twist in the Saga of the Kingdom

Every great story has a plot involving protagonists, antagonists, and a series of events leading up to a climax and an eventual conclusion. There is no greater story ever imagined than the saga of the Kingdom. In fact, every story of life takes part of its inspiration from this greatest of stories. God has gone to great lengths both to ensure that we can one day experience the life he intends for us and to make that life available to us even now. That is the story of the Kingdom.

We're all aware that life as we currently know it is not life as God fully intends. This disparity is explained by the story of the Garden of Eden. The Eden narrative establishes all the characters and elements of the greater human story.

Embedded in the creation account is an episode in which sin is introduced to the world. Evil, having already infiltrated the spiritual domain to challenge God's intentions, found a way into the earthly realm through the disobedience of Adam and Eve. Human beings, created in the image of God, had the power to choose good over evil. They chose poorly. The result of this pivotal decision, known as the Fall, disrupted (but did not derail) God's original design for life. At every level, from the subatomic to the cosmic, sin—insidious and pervasive—went to work against life.

Sin is anything that diminishes life. Any action or dynamic that undermines what is good and pure and right is sin, whether it originates with and is controlled by immediate agents or reverberates from some long-ago action that continues to affect God's good purposes. Because fullness of life is a gift from the King and a fundamental characteristic of the Kingdom, sin's competing agenda is bent on crippling and destroying the Kingdom by attacking life at its center. Sin damages and diminishes all life relationships, resulting in our estrangement from God, each other, ourselves, and Creation itself. Every personal evil results from sin, including egregious acts of violence, the quiet sabotage of others' opportunities, and the silent judgments we pass that consign others to a lesser status than we claim for ourselves.

The disruption caused by sin results in corporate complications, not just individual predicaments. From wars between nations to crimes against nature, the origin is the same. Society and culture embody profound life-diminishing forces that create and perpetuate poverty, injustice, prejudice, and inequality. The fact that generations of children worldwide are born into misery, oppression, and limited prospects for their lives provides a commentary on the tenacity of antilife once it gains a foothold. The inequitable distribution of resources and opportunity underscore the sinister effects of sin. A world in which injustice often goes unchallenged, restitution often goes neglected, and forgiveness often goes unpracticed points to the exponential impact of sin, which is further multiplied by its reach across decades and centuries.

Because life is not as God intended, we experience pain, frustration, anxiety, guilt, hatred—an entire range of toxic emotions. We treat ourselves and others poorly. We neglect God's desires and instructions. We violate the environment. These negative feelings and forces combine to create more evil as sin rampages against life.

Which brings us back to Eden, where we see a remarkable plot begin to unfold as God moves to protect the life he intends. Even as paradise was unraveling, God sprang into action. As death entered the Garden, he posted angelic sentinels to block access to the tree of life (Genesis 3:22-24). His action restricted the virus of antilife (sin) to keep it from overwhelming life. Evil would still play out its hand, resulting in death—evil's hard-earned wage. But life would ultimately triumph and become everlasting.

When we fast-forward to the end of Earth's story—as revealed in the book of Revelation—we learn that God's agenda has never changed. From Genesis on down to the final pages of human history, *life* is the point! Life was and is God's gift and goal, the signature expression of his Kingdom. In John's end-times vision of the city of God, as our present world is fully assimilated into the realized dream of God, we once again find a world with full and free access to life. "A river with the water of *life*" (Revelation 22:1) flows through the city. On each side grows "a tree of life" (22:2). Instead of a protected area in an abandoned paradise, access to the river and the tree of life is wide open in the city of God: "Let anyone who desires drink feely from the water of life" (22:17). The tree of life bears fruit all the time (22:2). The curse of sin is absent. Life is no longer compromised. "No longer will there be a curse upon anything" (22:3). The Kingdom of God will prevail: "The world has now become the Kingdom of our Lord and of his Christ" (11:15).

Breathtaking, isn't it?

Jesus and the Kingdom

Eden's story includes another stunning development. Rather than simply posting a guard at the tree of life and then retreating from the situation and abandoning his creation to the consequences of Adam and Eve's choices, God entered the fray, pitting himself against the forces that threaten life. In Genesis 3:15, the broad contours of a Kingdom

counteroffensive are outlined by God in his pronounce-
ment of judgment against the serpent. In a remarkable plot
twist, God revealed that he himself would one day become
a human being to demonstrate life as it was intended to be.

The culmination of that promise, the incarnation of Jesus
Christ, offers the clearest insight we have into the Kingdom
of God. Proclaiming the good news of the Kingdom was
Jesus' primary mission and message. In each New Testament
Gospel account, he comes onto the scene announcing that the
Kingdom "is near" (Matthew 4:17; Mark 1:15). Luke captures
Jesus' own understanding of his message and mission: "I must
proclaim the good news of the kingdom of God . . . because
that is why I was sent" (Luke 4:43, NIV). John puts it this way:
"The Word gave *life* to everything that was created, and his *life*
brought light to everyone" (John 1:4, italics added).

From Jesus, we learn the fundamental truth that the
Kingdom is God's primary activity on earth.

Jesus' Message

In his teaching, Jesus employed a treasure trove of metaphors to communicate various aspects and attributes of the
Kingdom of God. Here's a sampling from Matthew's Gospel,
with comments about the insight that each word picture
offers into the Kingdom.

- *A wedding feast* (Matthew 8:11; 22:2-10). In his
  description of a feast in the Kingdom of Heaven,
  Matthew emphasizes both the quality and diversity
  of the guest list, with mention of Abraham, Isaac,
  and Jacob and special emphasis on the inclusion of

Gentiles at the table. This would have shocked and scandalized his Jewish audience, who had been taught that the Kingdom belonged exclusively to them. In God's determination to fill the wedding hall with guests, we see his desire for joyful celebration, which characterizes the Kingdom atmosphere.

• *A seed-scattering farmer* (Matthew 13:3-9, 18-23). The farmer tosses seed indiscriminately on good and bad soil, prepared and unprepared ground, in hopes of a harvest. The full-throttled determination to get seed out, coupled with a hope for the seed's germination and growth, reflects God's attitude of abundant life.

• *A field of wheat and weeds* (Matthew 13:24-30, 36-43). Both the desirable wheat and the infiltrating weeds grow up together to be sorted out at harvest time; the reality of our present age is that two rival kingdoms cohabit in the same world and any attempt at premature "weeding" would limit the harvest.

• *A mustard seed* (Matthew 13:31-32). Something small grows into something big; the Kingdom is an expanding realm.

• *A little yeast* (Matthew 13:33). A small ingredient has a disproportionate impact as it penetrates the entire batch of dough. Likewise, the presence of the Kingdom infiltrates and influences every aspect of life.

• *A hidden treasure* (Matthew 13:44). An unexpected discovery is worth selling everything for; having the Kingdom is worth everything in life.

- *A valuable pearl* (Matthew 13:45-46). This time, the prize is sought after, not unexpectedly uncovered; yet the correct response is still to sell everything else to have it.

- *A fishing net* (Matthew 13:47-50). Fishing with a net always yields a mixed catch, requiring a later sorting out. A reality of God's Kingdom on earth is that both good and bad fish swim together, but in the end God will commission his angels to separate the evil from the righteous.

The above teachings relate to the Kingdom's present operation in the world. In the following stories, Jesus used other metaphors to illustrate the coming age of his Kingdom.

- *Ten bridesmaids* (Matthew 25:1-13). Some are prepared to enter the Kingdom; others are not.

- *Three servants* (Matthew 25:14-30). Celebration and reward come to those who invest in the Kingdom; those who squander life will lose it.

- *The final judgment* (Matthew 25:31-46). The King's criteria for allowing people to enter his Kingdom centers on whether they have improved people's lives by attending to their needs.

Jesus also challenged the prevailing notion of his day about who was favored in the Kingdom, upending the pecking order taught by first-century Judaism. Conventional wisdom said that the well-positioned and powerful, the affluent, and the religious were the people most favored by God. Jesus revealed that the greatest in the Kingdom are those who become "as humble as this little child" (Matthew 18:4). Rich people, Jesus said, would have a hard time entering the Kingdom (Matthew 19:23).

Jesus saved his harshest comments for the religious leaders. In a heated exchange with the chief priests and elders at the Temple, Jesus said, "Corrupt tax collectors and prostitutes will get into the Kingdom of God before you do" (Matthew 21:31). In that same discussion, Jesus likened these priests and elders to disobedient sons and wicked tenant farmers who would kill off the landowner's emissaries and even his son in an attempt to steal away the vineyard (Matthew 21:33-45). He warned them that "the Kingdom of God will be taken away from you" (Matthew 21:43).

However, if people were willing to adopt a different set of values, the Kingdom could be theirs. Jesus declared that the Kingdom belonged to the "poor in spirit" (Matthew 5:13) and to those "persecuted for doing right" (Matthew 5:10). Jews and Gentiles alike would be welcomed (Matthew 8:11). But he warned his disciples that "unless you turn from your sins and become like little children, you will never get into the Kingdom of Heaven" (Matthew 18:3), and he repeats this idea in Matthew 19:14.

Even the religious leaders were given hope if they were willing to make a huge adjustment in their focus. "Every teacher of religious law who becomes a disciple in the Kingdom of Heaven is like a homeowner who brings from his storeroom new gems of truth as well as old" (Matthew 13:52).

As we have seen, Jesus did not ignore issues of power,

authority, and inclusion when it came to discussions of the Kingdom. These concerns were high on the list of considerations then, and they still are for many people today. But Jesus radically redefined the landscape. The way of the Kingdom is a *spirit*, an *attitude*, and a *life* that honor God and allow us to serve as collaborators with him in helping others experience the life he intends for them.

This truth is nowhere more clearly revealed than in Jesus' comments about a pressing religious issue of his day. During the intertestamental period, many religious leaders came to believe that Israel's past captivities and exiles, along with their current subjugation by Rome, were punishments by God for their failure to observe the law of Moses. From this perspective grew the belief that if enough people would properly observe the law, especially the Sabbath ordinances, God would send his Messiah to earth to establish the Kingdom of God and restore Israel's prominent position among the nations of the earth. As a result of these views, the Jewish religious leaders had exponentially increased the number of observances and commandments for adherents to follow, as if by regulating every possible action the people's compliance with the law could be more precisely ascertained. Consequently, Pharisaic Judaism in the first century became both a burdensome, bewildering proposition for the common folk and a way to identify the truly pious—namely, the scribes and Pharisees. Jesus excoriated the religious leaders for this development, charging that "they crush people with unbearable religious demands and never lift a finger to ease the burden" (Matthew 23:4).

This is the backdrop, then, to the exchange between Jesus

and the religious leader who raised the question about which commandment was the most important. Jesus' consistent reply is recorded in all three synoptic Gospels (Matthew 22:37-40; Mark 12:28-31; Luke 10:25-28). He sums up the law (as well as the writings of the prophets) by telling us that we should love God with everything in ourselves and love our neighbors as ourselves. In Luke's account, Jesus illustrates the second part of this equation by telling the parable of the Good Samaritan. In Mark's version, a teacher of religious law says, "You have spoken the truth by saying that there is only one God and no other. And I know it is important to love him with all my heart and all my understanding and all my strength, and to love my neighbor as myself. This is more important than to offer all of the burnt offerings and sacrifices required in the law" (Mark 12:32-33). To this Jesus replies, "You are not far from the Kingdom of God" (Mark 12:34).

Jesus taught a straightforward concept of the Kingdom: people living the life that God intends and helping others enjoy the same opportunity.

Jesus' Mission

Jesus' message and mission were synonymous. The Kingdom of Heaven was not just something he talked about; he modeled it in his life, as well. His teachings on the Kingdom shaped the expression of his life and ministry. Jesus chided the religious leaders of his day for being hypocrites while he demonstrated what he taught by how he lived. The characterizations that we have just reviewed of what the Kingdom of God is like were part of Jesus' own life experience. He embodied the Kingdom in the way he lived.

- He was always the obedient child, deferring to his Father at every turn.

- He was a servant.

- He was poor.

- He was persecuted.

- He cast his message far and wide on good soil and soil that rejected his truth.

- He included among his followers people who did not initially believe and some who subsequently fell away.

- Tax collectors and prostitutes followed him.

- He gave all he had for the Kingdom—his own life—so that we could live.

- He transformed the Passover meal into a feast anticipating the Kingdom, saying, "I will not drink wine again until the day I drink it new in the Kingdom of God" (Mark 14:25).

- The miracles he worked backed up the message he preached. Everywhere Jesus went, the Kingdom broke into this world through his healings and other miracles.

- He outlived every obstacle, including death and the grave.

Jesus also made it abundantly clear that he was on a *life* mission. To an inquisitive Nicodemus, he declared that the point of God's sending his Son was to make available eternal life (John 3:16). To a hostile group of religious leaders he was crystal clear: "I tell you the truth, those who listen to my message and believe in God who sent me have eternal life. They will never be condemned for their sins, but they have already passed from death into life" (John 5:24). To genuine inquirers, he said, "I am the bread of life" (John 6:35). And to his closest followers, on their last night together before his crucifixion, he made a remarkable claim: "I am the way, the truth, and the life. No one can come to the Father except through me" (John 14:6). Jesus then left that gathering of disciples to complete his mission. Through his sacrificial and atoning death on the cross and his resurrection to life, he won and proved his victory: the power of life over death. He then ascended to heaven and will one day fulfill the very prayer he taught us to pray. The Kingdom *will* come in all its power and glory, and the *life* that God intends for all of us will be established forever.

Jesus' mission involved the invasion of another kingdom—the kingdom of Satan. This "kingdom of darkness" steals, maims, and destroys life. From its devastating entrance into our world through Eden, it has set up shop in every area of our lives to diminish God's intended design. The king of this dark kingdom offers a pale imitation of true life. But his is a kingdom under siege. Jesus made it plain that he came to wreak havoc on the kingdom of darkness. "For when a strong man like Satan is fully armed and guards his palace, his possessions are safe—until someone even stronger attacks and overpowers him, strips him of his weapons, and carries off his belongings" (Luke 11:21-22).

To punctuate his power over the world's strongman, Jesus engaged in a ministry of miracles. The variety and scope of Jesus' miraculous expressions demonstrated the breadth of his

Kingdom's domain. Meeting needs, binding up the broken-hearted, giving hope, setting people free from bondage of every kind—all are Kingdom enterprises. Jesus' miracles targeted physical needs (the feeding of the four thousand and the five thousand), physical restoration (curing the blind, the lame, and the sick), and spiritual bondage (casting out demons and calling tax collectors to repentance).

Each of these conditions addressed by Jesus' miracles was the result of sin (antilife), and each cure was a victory for the Kingdom of God. Jesus plainly made the connection between the two: "If I am casting out demons by the power of God, then the Kingdom of God has arrived among you" (Luke 11:20).

The tenor of Jesus' message and mission concerning the Kingdom emphasized its *immediacy*, *availability*, and *accessibility*. The first petition in the model prayer that Jesus taught his disciples was "May your Kingdom come soon" (Matthew 6:10). Then, to anchor the Kingdom as something concrete in the here-and-now, Jesus further instructed them (and us) to pray, "May your will be done on earth, as it is in heaven" (Matthew 6:10). He encouraged his disciples that they would not have to wrest the Kingdom away from God. Just the opposite was, and is, true. God is eager for us to experience the Kingdom. It is a gift: "It gives your Father great happiness to give you the Kingdom" (Luke 12:32).

However, we have a choice to self-select whether we want to be in or out of the Kingdom. Certainly, those who choose to do evil opt out (Luke 13:23-27). But we can also miss the Kingdom by not being diligent to pursue it. Jesus told his disciples to seek the Kingdom "above all else" (Matthew

6:33; Luke 12:31). The context for this instruction was Jesus' observation of his disciples' apparent anxiety over daily needs, including adequate food, drink, and clothing (Matthew 6:25; Luke 12:22-34). Jesus' admonition for them (and for us) was to seek the Kingdom *today*, not to view it as only a future destination beyond this life.

Life as God intends it is for *today*. The Kingdom is a present reality. Each moment on this earth, when we choose life over whatever diminishes life (sin), we participate in the Kingdom. We experience the Kingdom (already) come. We do what? We *live*! And we play our part in the heroic Kingdom narrative.

THE HEROIC KINGDOM NARRATIVE

ALL AROUND ME, I see evidence of the heroic Kingdom narrative being played out. Here are just a few examples of what I mean:

- A "bow tie" event, designed to break the Guinness world record for most bows being tied simultaneously and to raise money for a local benevolence ministry.

- A Jesus-follower in his late twenties, having quit his job in the business world to develop an after-school program in a drug- and crime-infested neighborhood, reports to his donors that more than three dozen kids are now being served every school day, plus weekends.

- A "million meal" pack-a-thon is being sponsored by a local food bank.

- A denominational faith group announces plans to collect one million books to supply every child in their state's school districts with up to five books to take home for summer reading.

- A program is announced allowing released prisoners a chance to learn vocational and life skills by working as interns in various local hospitality and service businesses.

- A bike rehabilitation plan at a local school fixes up bicycles so the homeless population can have a means of transportation to areas of the city not served by public transportation.

- A prominent businessman has been convening pastors of local congregations to spend time getting to know one another and to pray for their community. Now that some significant, prayerful relationships have developed, this community leader is proposing to move the group toward a plan of serving the community together as the body of Christ.

- An art auction benefits a family shelter.

- A congregation adopts a nearby elementary school in order to provide mentors, building and grounds beautification, and school supplies.

- A missional community creates a reading corner in the waiting area of a pediatric clinic.

- A symphony orchestra offers a concert of Brahms and Beethoven.

Some of these efforts involve the faith community. Many do not. Some are individual efforts, and others involve large organizations or collaborations between multiple groups. A number of the projects are administered by agencies that do ongoing work in these arenas, but many of the initiatives are the product of one person's passion or idea. What all of these efforts have in common, though, is this: people helping people to experience life as God intends it.

This has been the Kingdom story from the very beginning. Ever since Eden, God has been working to redeem and restore abundant life to people. It is a storyline that predates the church narrative. And it is a saga that will outlast the church.

In this chapter, we want to highlight key elements of the Kingdom narrative. We will build on some of our previous discussion, detailing truths that carry implications for our understanding of God's work in the world. If we don't know what to look for, the story can slip past us without our realizing it.

Kingdom Narrative Elements

Several aspects of the Kingdom story emerged from our discussion in chapter 2. These elements do not comprise the entire story but are some key points to keep in mind, especially if you are a church leader or Jesus-follower who wants to align your own story with the larger one that God is telling.

1. The Kingdom story is compelling because we are *living* it. All of us, when we were born, were cast headlong into the story of the Kingdom. We didn't ask for the roles we were given or beg to be here. But here we are. We seek to make sense of our lives because of a fundamental aspiration stamped into our essential being by our Designer. It is the yearning to experience the Kingdom—to have life as God intends for it to be.

This yearning fuels more than a hope. It causes us to believe that the life we seek is more than a dream—that it's a real-life possibility. This belief propels us out of our life-deficient circumstances to pursue the abundant life of the Kingdom. We work for it. We pray for it. We're not satisfied with the Kingdom remaining a distant, otherworldly reality. We want to see it manifested here on earth, just as it is in heaven. And it turns out that our desire is closely correlated with the heartbeat of God: He, too, wants to manifest the Kingdom here on earth!

The apostle Paul put it this way: "I press on to possess that perfection for which Christ Jesus first possessed me" (Philippians 3:12). Paul wanted to become the person that Jesus saw he could become when Jesus arrested him on the Damascus road. Even if we cannot express this idea as eloquently as Paul has, or with his spiritual precision, we know that this hope resides in every person on the planet—the dream to *really live*. That is the agenda of the Kingdom: to help people live into that dream.

We seek the Kingdom by aligning our lives with what we know about God's work in the world. He promised us that when we seek we will find. The reward for our search is *life*. That is the prize that keeps us pressing on.

2. The Kingdom of God is primarily a mission, not just a message. Ever since the Fall, God has been redeeming and restoring what was damaged in Eden—damage that extended far beyond the break in relationship between God and humanity. Sin (which we have defined as anything that diminishes life) negatively affects every realm of relationship: the lives we share with other people, the lives we share with the rest of the created order on our planet, and even the quality of life we experience within ourselves. God is working in each of these realms to restore life.

Jesus demonstrated God's mission during his life here on earth. He lived the mission of the Kingdom, bringing restoration and redemption everywhere he went, in all arenas of life. He performed miracles of physical healing, often linking them to matters of faith—"I haven't seen faith like this in all Israel!" (Luke 7:9)—and to emotional and psychological insight—"Would you like to get well?" (John 5:6). He demonstrated mastery over nature's elements—walking on water, commanding the wind, and turning water into wine. In his stories, such as the parable of the Prodigal Son, he addressed relational health. With the entire world in need of salvation, Jesus created a tight community of a dozen close friends to demonstrate the importance of our belonging to one another.

The missional church conversation of the past two decades has drawn attention to the bedrock Kingdom truth that *mission* is central to the Kingdom. This emphasis comes after centuries in which the church has focused primarily on getting the *message* right (which was a natural outgrowth of the doctrinal concerns that powered the Reformation). Now the shift is underway to getting the mission right.

The gospel is the good news of the Kingdom: Life as God

intended it is available. Sharing the gospel means much more than passing along information about securing personal salvation and asking for assent. Living the truth, not just speaking the truth, is the acid test of authenticity. So, we can *say* that Jesus brings fullness of life, and that's certainly true; but as his ambassadors, what are we *doing* to facilitate fullness of life for the people in our spheres of influence?

3. All efforts that enhance life as God intends are Kingdom efforts. This truth is a corollary to the perspective that the Kingdom is primarily a God-initiated mission to restore the life he intends us to have. Helping a child learn to read, providing clean drinking water, eradicating disease, creating jobs, alleviating suffering and pain, delivering health care to people, raising children to become responsible life-enhancing adults—all of these efforts are Kingdom endeavors. Likewise, seeking peace, protecting the environment, working to reduce poverty, tackling prejudice and discrimination, and challenging systems that create and perpetuate family dysfunction are also part of the Kingdom saga. Enhancing people's lives and promoting beauty through music, art, drama, and literature are worthy Kingdom efforts. So is the profound work of helping people recapture their rightful spiritual identity as human beings—image bearers of the King.

Simply put, every good deed and expression of goodwill points to the Kingdom. The pervasive presence of good reflects a breaking-in of the Kingdom of God, advancing against the kingdom of antilife.

An intriguing recent development in our culture supports this subplot in the Kingdom storyline. It is the emergence of *service* as a core value of the millennial generation. These younger adults have grown up participating in all kinds of community service and development projects as part of their school curricula and extracurricular activities. I'm not talking only about church youth groups undertaking mission projects at home and overseas. I'm talking about nonchurch activities as well, such as when the workers at LensCrafters journey to third-world countries to recycle eyewear,[1] or when college fraternities and sororities donate time and money to construct family shelters or participate in other community service initiatives.[2]

These young people—Jesus-followers and others—share a conviction that they should contribute to good causes. Two local young men I spoke with a couple of years ago promote microeconomic development in West African villages by selling West African–made clothes on their marketing website. Many millennials support businesses whose corporate altruism aligns with their personal interests. They buy shoes so that others with no shoes can get a pair. They are the first in their organizations to volunteer vacation time to travel to places of need around the world. Millennials fill the ranks of disaster-relief teams. They are eager to provide foster care for underprivileged kids in the United States and to adopt kids from other countries in order to rescue them from their poverty. They sometimes sacrifice career advancement by taking time to join the Peace Corps or participate in programs such as Teach for America.

One young couple I met has chosen to live as community development missionaries. Through their work with the Christian Community Development Association (CCDA), they are offering their lives to revitalize an inner city in the South.[3] They moved their family into the worst neighborhood of their city in an effort to bring some health into brokenness. Others are joining them in an attempt to create an island of health to build on and expand throughout the neighborhood. This couple and their cohorts are a Kingdom assault team.

4. **People who do good by enhancing life contribute to the Kingdom enterprise, even if they are unaware of it.** Classic examples of this truth can be found in both the Old and New Testaments. In the Old Testament, God refers to Cyrus, king of Persia, as "my shepherd" for his role in releasing the people of Israel from Babylonian captivity and repatriating them to their homeland in Palestine (Isaiah 44:28). Cyrus would hardly have called his military campaign against Babylon a Kingdom of God "shepherding" initiative. However, what he did played right into God's agenda. Similarly, in the New Testament parable of the Good Samaritan, the unsuspecting hero of the story takes time to help another human being who is in trouble. That's the Kingdom in action.

This dynamic still holds true today. A person seeking a cure for cancer, or representing people who can't afford to hire legal aid, or helping at-risk kids, or working to create sustainable farming methods, or developing software to help people communicate better—or pursuing a gazillion other endeavors—engages in the Kingdom agenda. The entire breadth of activities that improve human and planetary conditions can qualify as Kingdom exploration and expression.

5. **The truth that advancing the Kingdom is God's primary activity on earth carries enormous implications for**

the church. This reality should cause us to reconsider both the kinds of activities we engage in and the focus that the church should bring to all its efforts.

Recently, I met with a group of community leaders in a city of about 300,000 people. They convened the gathering as part of an effort by a faith-based organization to build a cross-domain collaborative (an effort involving people from various sectors of a community working together to achieve a common objective) to address some key issues in their city. The assembly had representatives from government, education, business, health-care, law-enforcement, media, religious, and social sectors. At the meeting, the recently elected mayor gave an impromptu and impassioned speech about why he had moved back to his hometown after going away to school and enjoying career success in another part of the country. This young businessman-turned-politician was not a person of faith, and he had no idea that he had made some very serious Kingdom work possible. But his spirit—and particularly his remarks to the group that day—opened the door and paved the way for the faith-based initiative to gain traction throughout the city. The education and health-care initiatives that emerged from this community-wide collaboration will improve the lives of many people across the entire region.

6. The King is able to use more than just acts of goodness to expand his Kingdom and further his agenda; he also routinely turns the tables on the kingdom of antilife, flipping the enemy's strategies into Kingdom advances. The Bible makes this point often. One clear example is Joseph's story in Genesis 37–50. In an act of betrayal by his jealous brothers, Joseph was sold into slavery and carried to Egypt. However, this misdeed was used by God to place Joseph in a place of power and influence in Egyptian society. There, his wisdom and skills enabled the region to avoid the calamity of mass starvation. Joseph's food storage program prepared the Egyptians to survive in the face of a massive famine. Many people who would have starved to death were spared. All this came to pass because Joseph's foresight and administrative genius had been made available to Pharaoh, courtesy of an evil plot years earlier.

In an ironic twist of circumstances, Joseph's brothers came to him for food. In confronting them and revealing his identity to them, he summed up God's ability to bring good out of evil: "You intended to harm me, but God intended it all for good. He brought me to this position so I could save the lives of many people" (Genesis 50:20). The brothers' evil act wound up saving their own skins. Only a King like God could pull that off.

We see the same dynamic in the life of Jesus. The plot to eliminate him, hatched by Judas and the religious leaders, set into motion the events leading up to the Crucifixion. However, Satan, the great deceiver operating behind the scenes, became ensnared by his own evil plans. Instead of putting an end to Jesus, the Cross accomplished God's Kingdom agenda on earth, opening the way for all things to be redeemed and restored. And instead of sealing Jesus away, the grave became the backdrop for the Resurrection, which sounded the death knell for death and signaled the inevitable destruction of the kingdom of antilife. The empty tomb declared that the rival kingdom will not stand. It's over!

The victory has been won. Now we are in the process of releasing the captives.

We hear the same Kingdom-prevailing dynamic every time someone tells the story of how calamity helped to forge their character and move them closer to God. Every turned-around life testifies to the subversive activity of the Kingdom of God as it upsets the prevailing world order. Every whisper of hope that suggests the possibility of a better life carries with it the refrain of the Kingdom. Even our own deaths become portals of entry into the Kingdom that God has prepared for us.

7. **The Kingdom agenda belongs to the King, not to us.** God alone knows what he is up to in any given situation. There is no way that Joseph, strapped to the back of a Midianite camel, could have known that his unplanned and to-all-appearances disastrous situation would be used by God to eventually save the very family members who had just sold Joseph into slavery. Nor could the disciples, witnessing Jesus' crucifixion, understand the implications of his sacrifice for all humanity. This reality is comforting for all of us who frequently find ourselves in situations where fear and despair seem to have the upper hand. The eventual outcome is not in doubt, we know. But we can also know "that God causes everything to work together for the good of those who love God and are called according to his purpose for them" (Romans 8:28). Why is this so? Because God is inexorably working for his Kingdom to be established. This perspective highlights the truth that it is not only God's ability but also his determination that gives us confidence that he is always working his Kingdom agenda. This dual awareness provides

the grounding for our sure knowledge that "if God is for us, who can ever be against us?" (Romans 8:31).

As I write these lines, the world has recently celebrated the life and contributions of Nelson Mandela, a celebration occasioned by Mandela's death at the age of ninety-five. *Celebration* seems the most appropriate word to describe the world's reaction to Mandela's passing. Who does not know at least some of his remarkable story? He grew up in the era of apartheid and was unjustly imprisoned for years for his work to end the institution of cultural and racial discrimination. However, the anti-apartheid protest movement for which he was jailed was too powerful to confine behind bars. Mandela saw the end of apartheid and emerged from prison to become the president of his nation. He publicly forgave his prison guards and set about working for racial and cultural reconciliation. His life matched his message. So many aspects of his Kingdom influence grew directly from the hostility and unjust persecution he had endured. God turned evil into good: Kingdom dynamics in action.

8. Kingdom timelines and storylines run longer than a single human lifespan. Sometimes it takes centuries to close the loop on redemptive subplots in the larger Kingdom storyline.

When Nebuchadnezzar overran Jerusalem, Israel's forced march into captivity in Babylon positioned the young prophet Daniel to eventually become a chief advisor to the Babylonian ruler. Through his influence in the royal court, Daniel introduced the worship of the Most High God into Babylonian culture. It is no wonder, then, that the wise men who came to Jerusalem centuries later in pursuit of the newborn King of the Jews came from Babylon. There is no way Daniel could have known that his actions set the stage for key characters to be added to our Nativity sets! The events he set in motion carried implications far beyond his own lifetime.

Nor could the apostle Paul have known that his turning away from Asia to travel to Europe on his second missionary trip would alter the course of Western civilization. Nor could Martin Luther have envisioned that his sermon notes would start a movement that would change the face of Christendom. The list can go on and on. The impact of our lives cannot always be measured in a single lifetime.

The King has scripted our parts and our lives into the larger Kingdom story, which began long before our arrival on the planet and will continue after our departure. This perspective gives rise to hope and faith on our part. Our job is to be obedient, to play our respective roles. The King's job involves plot development and cast support.

In none of this discussion do I intend to imply that you and I are mere cogs in a machine or puppets in a marionette-theater production. Our capacity to choose, to opt in or out, remains central to who we are as creatures bearing the divine image. We're free to decide whether to accept our assignments and deliver our lines. Our marveling at the greatness of God increases when we realize that he deals with our choices as part of the continuing Kingdom saga. He constantly weaves multiple life lines throughout each scene.

God desires our obedience and our joyful participation, but the success of his agenda doesn't depend on our decisions or efforts. There are contingencies we don't know anything about and couldn't fathom even if we did. For instance, if Paul had not accepted his assignment as an apostle, we can be certain that God would have used another option. The proper response to the realization that God doesn't *need* us, but that he has chosen us to be his Kingdom agents, is humility and gratitude that we've been allowed to partner with God in whatever he is up to. Nowhere is there room for pride, as if we've been chosen for roles that only we can play. Our concern should be not missing out on the roles we've been given to play in the great story of the Kingdom.

9. The Kingdom of God is making great progress. The Kingdom is secure. The Kingdom is always expanding, always growing, always invading and challenging the kingdom of darkness. Jesus declared that the gates of hell would not prevail against the onslaught of the Kingdom. As we have seen, he likened the expansion of the Kingdom to the growth of a mustard seed and the pervasive influence of yeast in bread. These images rule out any idea of retreat. Leonard Sweet, an author friend of mine, wonders why church leaders go on "retreats," so he holds "advances" instead. That's the Kingdom spirit!

We should understand that, when we align our lives with God's Kingdom efforts, we're joining a winning cause. Throwing our lot in with the Kingdom always pays dividends well beyond our expectations. When I congratulated one elderly gentleman on the impact he has had on the life of the high-school boy that he mentors, he told me, with tears streaming down his cheeks, "What he's doing for me is far more than I am doing for him." That sentiment expresses Kingdom dynamics: both parties blessed; both lives changed.

As Kingdom agents, we should never adopt a siege mentality, as if the Kingdom of God were under attack. No! Through the power and guidance of the Holy Spirit, we're bringing the fight to the enemy. Some Christians want to hunker down, assuming a posture of protection, preservation, and withdrawal from a world they view as hostile. When church leaders and congregations operate from this worldview, the church becomes a cloister, a place in which to hide from the world rather than engage with it. But the Kingdom of God is not a hiding place, a defensive fortress, or a way to separate ourselves from the world—because the Kingdom of God is not under siege.

The Kingdom represents an invasion, an aggressive and tireless campaign for engaging with the world and driving back the forces of darkness. Having a Kingdom mind-set propels us constantly into the world, where we make nonstop forays into enemy territory, doing as much good as we can, always determined to carry out rescue missions in order to diminish the territory of darkness and spread the life that God intends for as many people as possible.

A Kingdom mentality is what causes a woman like Jenny Williamson to contend against sex trafficking. Once she became aware of the prevalence of this evil in her community, she began to facilitate action among law enforcement, state agencies, the faith community, businesses, and schools to tackle the causes as well as the consequences of this horrific antilife plague on humanity. Though raising awareness of human trafficking is a vital part of what Jenny does, and it plays a critical role in mobilizing forces to confront this evil in our society, Jenny hasn't stopped there. Instead, she has begun constructing Courage Houses, which provide young women a safe place of escape and long-term recovery when they decide to make a break from the prison of sexual exploitation. One girl and one situation at a time, she is charging the gates of hell and raiding the devil's storehouse, knowing that she is on the winning side. The idea of retreat or withdrawal never crosses her mind.[4]

10. The Kingdom involves celebration. Jesus preached the Kingdom as *good news*. He likened it to a banquet, a feast, a party—all scenarios involving joy and abundance. And why not? The Kingdom is winning, expanding, looking forward to a secure and victorious outcome. This means we can celebrate, regardless of our immediate circumstances or surroundings. As David said, God prepares for us a feast to enjoy, even "in the presence of [our] enemies" (Psalm 23:5).

Kingdom people are free to enjoy, free to bless, free to affirm, free to be persistent and patient, free to serve, free to love, and free to live! Living the abundant life that God intends for us proves to be infectious and attractive to people looking for a way out of darkness, where an atmosphere of uncertainty, skepticism, and cynicism generates constant discouragement and sense of loss.

The early church possessed this attitude, which enabled early followers of Jesus to live out a compelling story that won over an empire. They attracted attention and adherents not through abrasive confrontation but through acts of love and service. By rescuing abandoned babies off the doorsteps of Roman homes, for example, and by staying behind in the cities to care for the sick when plagues ravaged the population, they presented an appealing alternative lifestyle to the self-absorbed, indulgent, and impious world of ancient Rome.

A friend of mine hosts block parties for his neighborhood as a way to promote celebration in a world that can knock people down. Over time, he has had opportunities to speak into the lives of people who are drawn to him and trust him because of his obvious love for life.

Contrast this example with the street preacher I encountered outside an upscale mall in downtown, down-under Sydney. Perched on a pedestal, he screamed "bad news" into a microphone. His main message focused on hell, and a placard propped up beneath him posed the question, "Is a moment of sinful pleasure on earth worth spending an eternity in the flames of hell?" People stopped only to witness the weirdness and to shake their heads in derision and disbelief. The only message that came through was one of judgment, condemnation, disfavor, and condescension. The man's message and manner of delivery had no hint of the Kingdom. His approach was not only unattractive and uncompelling—it was actually repulsive. It was religion at its worst.

11. The battle between the kingdoms of good and evil will not go on forever. The onslaught of the Kingdom of God against the kingdom of darkness has a distinct and certain timeline. The parable of the wheat and the weeds (Matthew 13:24-30) teaches that, although the good is intermingled with the not-good for a season, the two will be separated at the harvest. Similarly, the parable of the foolish and wise bridesmaids (Matthew 25:1-13) carries the message that there will come a time when entrance into the Kingdom is no longer possible for the unprepared. Apparently, it is possible to be "cast out" or to miss out on the Kingdom. In every case, those who fall into this category are characterized as evildoers, lovers of darkness who resist the light, and perpetrators of antilife. "Nothing evil will be allowed to enter, nor anyone who practices shameful idolatry and dishonesty—but only those whose names are written in the Lamb's Book of Life" (Revelation 21:27). This outcast group finds further definition in the following passage of Revelation: "Outside the city are the dogs—the sorcerers, the sexually immoral, the murderers, the idol worshipers, and all who love to live a lie" (Revelation 22:15).

The subject of hell—what it is, who will go there, and whether it is eternal or eventually destroyed—is not the focus of our discussion. However, we cannot ignore the reality of hell and still do justice to the biblical witness. Suffice it to say that the Kingdom of God eventually vanquishes the rival kingdom that maims and steals away the life that God intends for us. At that time, God will usher in his fully realized, victorious, and unchallenged Kingdom.

12. The Kingdom of God on earth points to the ultimate destination for humanity. Proofs for the eternal Kingdom's existence can be seen in the outcroppings of Kingdom life that break into this present world. George Eldon Ladd, a twentieth-century evangelical scholar, wrote extensively about the idea that the Kingdom is "already, but not yet."[5] Jesus taught us to pray that the will of God would be done on earth as it is in heaven. He tied this to the prayer that the Kingdom of God would *come*. This means that, each time the will of God is done on earth, the Kingdom becomes a present reality. This truth motivates followers of Jesus to partner with

God in his redemptive mission on earth. It also encourages us to take heart each time that life triumphs over the diabolical forces of antilife. Each victory serves as evidence that the full manifestation of the Kingdom is on its way. Kingdom living is not a way of life that will be available only in eternity. God intends us to experience it today.

A Compelling Story

This, then, is the heroic Kingdom narrative: God is at work in the world today, redeeming and restoring life to its intended design. These efforts stretch across all domains of human endeavor. Everyone has the opportunity to get in on God's Kingdom agenda; not just a select few. When we pursue the abundant life that Jesus promised, we find ourselves aligned with the forces of heaven and good. All efforts to improve people's lives count, even though we may not see the full impact we make when we partner with God's Kingdom agenda. Living this way is rewarding, yielding benefits to us as well as to those who are helped by our efforts.

The fact that people strive to better the lives of others, even sometimes in the face of certain death, reveals just how powerful the Kingdom of God is. The idea that things can be better, that life can be improved, that people can become more of who they can be, is the hope implanted in the human heart by our God and King.

In the poem "O Me! O Life!" Walt Whitman laments the seeming contradictions and shortcomings of all human experience, culminating in the plaintive question, "What good amid these, O me, O life?" But then Whitman answers his own questions: "That you are here—that life exists and

identity, that the powerful play goes on, and you may contribute a verse."[6]

Where would an idea like that come from? I suggest that
it is anchored in the story of the Kingdom that pervades
human consciousness and history. Reminding people of
these truths is the task of God's people. This is the story
we're supposed to tell. The Kingdom saga is compelling and
beats the heck out of any other substitute narrative—even if
the competition comes from the church!

CHALLENGING THE CHURCH'S STORYLINE

A HALF-DOZEN REPRESENTATIVES OF various Christian denominational tribes had convened to figure out how to launch a literacy initiative in their city together. The project was described
by the collaborators as an expression of the faith community.
Toward the end of the meeting, someone raised the question
of whether non-Christian faith groups would be invited to
partner in the effort. No decisions were made, but several
comments offered around the table indicated a consensus that
leaned toward adopting an inclusive approach rather than
limiting project participants exclusively to Christian groups.

When the meeting broke up, one of the participants hung
back so he could have a word with me. This denominational
executive expressed his concern.

"I'm not sure about this all-inclusive approach involving Hindus, Muslims, Buddhists, whomever," he said.

"Why?" I asked him.

"Because, to me, the Cross is central to everything," he replied. "I'm interested in doing this because Christ motivates me."

I reminded him that the group had purposely decided that this literacy campaign would be an expression of the faith community, not a campaign to build the faith community disguised as a literacy effort. "We aren't doing this to build church attendance," I said.

He nodded. "That's right."

I probed a bit further. "Do you see this as a Kingdom agenda rather than a church agenda?"

I explained that, in my view, helping kids learn to read was essential to helping them experience abundant life—like Jesus helping the blind to see and the lame to walk.

"I know all that," he replied. "I just don't know if I can keep our pastors at the table if this is a cooperative effort with people of other faiths."

As he left, I thought to myself: *This is symptomatic of the story confusion plaguing the American church.* Presented with a clear Kingdom agenda—creating an opportunity for more abundant life to break out in his community—this leader was unbelievably reluctant to join in. His position seemed to suggest that cooperating with other faiths in Kingdom enterprise is a questionable activity for church leaders. Whatever the reason for his allergic reaction to the literacy campaign, he felt that it was acceptable for church concerns to trump Kingdom responsibilities. How would the Christian movement ever have gotten off the ground with that kind of thinking? I wondered how he would have reacted if I had suggested that we might find ourselves reading to kids alongside agnostics and atheists.

I recently sat in on a meeting with a group of church leaders who were planning a collaborative project to collect and distribute more than thirty thousand books for a summer reading program among the students in the city's school district. The woman making the presentation remarked at the end, "While we are helping kids to read, our real hope is that they become disciples of Jesus through this effort."

Another member of the group spoke up and said, "We need to help kids learn to read because God wants them to have a good shot at life. We don't need to do this project as a way to open the door for evangelism. This is a Kingdom effort, and we need to do it because we are Kingdom people, trusting the Spirit with whatever else he wants to do through it."

I don't think the presenter was approaching the project with an ulterior motive. However, I think the exchange helped the group clarify its intentions and values. What was instructive to me was her perceived need to defend a Kingdom initiative—to a group of church people! It was almost as if she felt compelled to salute the flag or recite her allegiance to the cause. It was as if helping kids learn to read better did not have enough merit of its own, so the project needed to be legitimized by a stated evangelistic aspiration.

Until we get the relationship between Kingdom and church rightly sorted, we will continue to practice a church-centered

Christianity that is detrimental to the Kingdom. We will continue to work against the Lord's Prayer sentiment that the Kingdom show up on earth!

Church and Kingdom

Matthew records the only three uses of the word *church* in the Gospels. The first is embedded in a conversation between Jesus and his disciples, when he asks them what people were saying about him.

> When Jesus came to the region of Caesarea Philippi, he asked his disciples, "Who do people say the Son of Man is?"
>
> They replied, "Some say John the Baptist; others say Elijah; and still others, Jeremiah or one of the prophets."
>
> "But what about you?" he asked. "Who do you say I am?"
>
> Simon Peter answered, "You are the Messiah, the Son of the living God."
>
> Jesus replied, "Blessed are you, Simon son of Jonah, for this was not revealed to you by flesh and blood, but by my Father in heaven And I tell you that you are Peter, and on this rock I will build my church, and the gates of Hades will not overcome it. I will give you the keys of the kingdom of heaven; whatever you bind on earth will be bound in heaven, and whatever you loose on earth will be loosed in heaven." (Matthew 16:13-19, NIV)

The disciples would have been very familiar with the term *church* (*ekklesia*). It is a word that simply means *assembly*. With this declaration, Jesus announced that he was creating his own assembly—of people who recognized him for who he was.

The assembly (church) of disciples would receive the keys of the Kingdom of Heaven. Many scholars suggest that the image here is of a faithful household steward, who would carry keys to open and to lock up (Isaiah 22:20-22). Others suggest that the phrase refers to a rabbinical term designating the office of the scribe: a teacher of the law of God. What all would agree on, however, is that being given the keys of the Kingdom represents the granting of authority and steward-ship. This means that the world should be able to count on the church to deliver Kingdom instruction and demonstrate Kingdom activity.

The Kingdom agenda—life as God intends it—is supposed to be the church's agenda. The church's narrative is supposed to be Kingdom-centric. When the church doesn't point to the Kingdom, it abandons its true colors and becomes something other than the church that Jesus established. Simply put, a congregation in the church business instead of the people (life) business is on slippery ground. No matter how sincerely we might believe that our self-contained and self-absorbed church activities honor God's design for his gathered people, such expressions of church are more likely to impede God's mission than advance it. When the church flies non-Kingdom colors, no matter how winsome or attractive they may be, it sets itself in competition with the Kingdom and becomes a bastion of Churchianity rather than Christianity. Jesus' warning to the religious leaders of his day, though issued in a separate context, should nonetheless be taken seriously: "I tell you, the Kingdom of God will be taken away from you and given to a nation that will produce the proper fruit" (Matthew 21:43). In my opinion, contemporary Christianity is no more immune to this judgment than was the version of Judaism that had perverted the mission of the Kingdom in Jesus' day.

Sadly, there is plenty of evidence to suggest we are in danger at this point.

Signs of Church-Centeredness

In North America, Christianity is viewed largely as a church-centered practice, yielding an organization that is religious but not necessarily reflective of God's desires for his people. The prevailing perspective in far too many congregations is a misguided view of the nature and role of the church in God's mission. Not only is it unbiblical, but it also undermines, distorts, and discredits God's Kingdom agenda.

Here are just a few examples of church-centered thinking and practice that have become so ensconced in church culture that they seem normal. The fact that many church folks who read this list will wonder, *What's the big deal?* only underscores how ingrained these perspectives have become. We have practiced church this way for so long that we don't even question these things anymore.

- The prevailing concept of church as a *place* associated with a particular set of activities (worship, Bible study, etc.)—that is, as an *it*, not a *who*.

- A scorecard for success based largely on church activities led by church people for church people, primarily on church property.

- A pervasive consumer mentality whereby a church congregation is evaluated on the strength and quality of its programming.

- A misguided sense of purpose—seeing "building the church" as God's primary mission in the world.

- A deliberate and detailed focus on the mechanics of "doing church" (e.g., *What kind of worship services will we offer? How will we attract people to our activities? How are we different or better than other churches?*).

- A clergy (church leadership) trained to manage an institution (real estate, budgets, etc.) and produce religious goods and services (sermons, programs, religious rites).

- A membership trained to "give to the church" their talents, time, and treasure, and whose spirituality is assessed according to their participation in church activities, which is seen as "supporting the church."

- Church resources spent primarily on buildings, staff, and church-based programs, with much lower priority given to alleviating human need and suffering.

- Assessments of members' spiritual gifts typically linked to church-centered expressions of service.

- Church members' expectations or assumptions that it is "the church's job" to provide spiritual training and nurture for their children.

- The inability of many church people to have in-depth conversations about God, even with their spouses and children. Instead, they have conversations about church that largely reflect consumer issues: "How did you like the service?" "What did you think of the pastor's sermon?" "Are you planning to attend the youth event this weekend?" These are participation-in-church-activities discussions, not discipleship or spiritual-growth conversations.

- The inability of many church people to have spiritual conversations with non–church people. Church people often know how to talk about church (typically a conversation about a church activity) but not about God or his Kingdom priorities. People in our culture want to have God conversations, not church conversations.

- The Ephesians 4 list of Jesus' gifts to the church (apostle, prophet, evangelist, pastor, teacher) being used to designate roles and offices connected to institutional church roles and offices.

- The use of the word *parachurch*, which implies that only what happens in an institutional church context counts as real church.

- A T-shirt-and-bumper-sticker theology that says it all: "I love my church"; "Follow me to church"; "This is my church"; "A place where [fill in the blank]."

"Houston, we have a problem."

Just as NASA's scientists were faced with a threat to

the lives of the Apollo 13 astronauts when a system failure allowed the development of a toxic environment aboard the spacecraft, the church faces a toxic environment of its own creation, brought about by a failure to understand its true mission. The mission itself and the spiritual lives of the people involved are at stake.

In the case of Apollo 13, the NASA scientists engineered a solution to keep the crew's own carbon dioxide emissions (their exhaled breath) from killing them. We have a similar problem in the church. We need a solution to save us from ourselves.

Fortunately, as was the case with Apollo 13, the elements needed to fix the problem are already at hand. But we need to seriously recalibrate the relationship between the church and the Kingdom.

Kingdom Correctives

In order to synchronize the church's story with the Kingdom narrative, three critical shifts in our perspective are necessary.

1. We must recognize that God established the church to point to the Kingdom, not the other way around. We shouldn't be trying to promote the church; we should be trying to raise awareness of the Kingdom. After all, the church touches only a portion of what God is up to in the world. He is working in all arenas of human endeavor to advance his Kingdom so that people can experience life as he intends it. This work of redeeming and restoring what was lost in Eden is God's major work in the world. As such, the Kingdom—not the church—is the focal point of God's ultimate designs on earth.

This perspective should markedly influence how the church intersects with the world. For starters, we should approach the Kingdom endeavor with a strong dose of humility because we often don't really know what God is up to at any particular place or time. Instead of engaging our communities from an imperialistic perspective (getting them onto our agenda—whether that's evangelistic, political, social, or otherwise), we should take a seat at the table as one of the players and make room for the King himself to initiate, guide, empower, and produce what *he* wants to accomplish.

Let me give you an example of how this shift in emphasis can play out. Recently, in one of our major metropolitan areas, a multi-church group conducted a campaign to "bless the city," complete with goals and strategies designed to have an impact on some big issues, particularly education and health care. Unfortunately, the "bless the city" initiative fell victim to a church-centered mind-set. All the efforts were explicitly labeled as church initiatives, dreamed up and executed by church people "for the good of the city." I know this was a well-intentioned effort, and I celebrate the good that came out of it; but it came across as another church program to call attention to the church, with any positive results already chalked up to the church's credit.

Pointing to the church is the wrong storyline. The effort smacked of hubris: "We're bringing God into the equation. We know what's good for you, and we're going to give it to you."

A Kingdom-focused approach would be conceived and implemented differently. It would involve lots of listening and local input and would be conducted from a posture of quiet service, rather than trying to send a "we're here to bless you" message, which can seem self-serving. It would operate from a conviction that God is already at work in the city. It would raise awareness that God wants the city to prosper and that, as God's people, we want to help. God would be the star of the show, and his will that the Kingdom come on earth would be the main message. Such a shift in perspective involves more than just another marketing strategy. It provides a different narrative altogether for the effort, as the church points to the Kingdom, rather than to itself.

2. We must acknowledge that the Kingdom, not the church, is the destination. I often use the analogy of an airport to clarify the distinction between Kingdom and church. An airport is not designed to be a destination. No one plans a vacation to hang out at the airport or to take in the sights at their nearest transportation hub. In fact, when people have to spend more time at the airport than they planned, they usually aren't happy about it. The airport's job is to get people to *somewhere else* as quickly and efficiently as possible. That doesn't mean the airport is unimportant—not at all! In fact, a properly functioning airport is crucial to the journey's success. But the airport is not the point of the trip. The airport is not the destination. And no airport can hold a candle to the destination that prompted the journey in the first place.

I'm sure you can see where this is going. The church is not the destination, and it's not the point of the journey. It's the life of the Kingdom that we're trying to get to. That's what people are after. That's what the trip is all about. When we keep people hanging around at the church too long, we're taking them off-mission and messing up their journey. And when we suggest that what happens at the church is the point of the trip, we supplant their destination aspirations. That doesn't mean the church is unimportant—not at all! A properly functioning church is often crucial to the advancement of the Kingdom. But the church is a poor substitute for the Kingdom.

Consider another analogy from a Japanese student I mentored in an online course. He went into considerable detail about his work as an apprentice in his career path, on his way to becoming a journeyman and then, finally, fully credentialed in his trade. He asked me if I thought the role of the church should be similar to that of apprenticeship and coaching for full deployment in the Kingdom as "fully credentialed" followers of Jesus. I think that's a great insight. The church should be our tutor, helping us to master the skills we need to grow in our competency and character as disciples. The apostle Paul strikes the same chord in his letter to the Ephesians:

> Christ himself gave the apostles, the prophets,
> the evangelists, the pastors and teachers, to equip
> his people for works of service, so that the body
> of Christ may be built up until we all reach unity
> in the faith and in the knowledge of the Son of
> God and become mature, attaining to the whole
> measure of the fullness of Christ.
>
> Then we will no longer be infants, tossed back
> and forth by the waves, and blown here and there
> by every wind of teaching and by the cunning and
> craftiness of people in their deceitful scheming.

Instead, speaking the truth in love, we will grow to
become in every respect the mature body of him
who is the head, that is, Christ. From him the whole
body, joined and held together by every supporting
ligament, grows and builds itself up in love, as each
part does its work. (Ephesians 4:11-16, NIV)

In far too many churches, the program seems designed to
keep people from ever "graduating." Rather than celebrating
growth and development into deployment, we have created
a culture that doesn't expect people to "become mature,
attaining to the whole measure of the fullness of Christ,"
which means embodying Christ in the world, advancing
the Kingdom. We need churches that are dedicated to the
objective of helping people *grow up* in the faith, so they can
live *on mission* in the world, to see their lives as a mission
trip. Instead, in far too many cases, we keep 'em comin'
back for the same thing every week, figuring out ways to
pique their interest, giving them church jobs to make them
feel "involved," making it seem normal to become sophisti-
cated church-service consumers—and calling all this a sign
of maturity.

If we rightly understand that the Kingdom is the destination, we will figure out ways to celebrate spiritual progress on the journey that leads people to full deployment as
Kingdom agents.

This is one of those times when I must plead, "Please
don't hear what I'm *not* saying." I'm not suggesting that
people should leave the church, or that church is just for
kids (or spiritual infants), or that people don't need ongoing

instruction and support in their spiritual development and life journeys. What I *am* saying is that we can do better than to keep people repeating the same grade year after year—"always learning but never able to come to a knowledge of the truth" (2 Timothy 3:7, NIV)—with no *next* for them in Kingdom assignment and accountability. But unless we realize that the real game is *real life*—not artificial *church* life—we won't be motivated to figure this out.

3. We must realize that the Kingdom saga focuses primarily on the welfare of the community, not on the church. A Kingdom perspective means that the cues for authentic church celebration come from the quality of life that people experience in the world, beyond the church. All my life, the mantra among church leaders has been something akin to this: *If we will just build great churches, we will have great cities.* This "trickle out" theory for community development begins—and all too often ends—at the church, and it has given rise to all sorts of efforts over the past several decades that have resulted in lots of great church facilities stocked with great programming options. The net result has been bigger congregations with fantastic programs, exquisite worship experiences, and impressive facilities. But better cities? Hardly. Disaffection toward church participation? Rising. Discernible Kingdom advances? Hardly enough!

We've had it backwards. Listen to the instructions that Jeremiah gave to the exiles in Babylon. After telling the people they should make a home in their alien surroundings (rather than hunkering down with a siege mentality), the prophet relays the following instructions from God: "Work for the peace and prosperity of the city where I sent you into exile. Pray to the LORD for it, for *its welfare will determine your welfare*" (Jeremiah 29:7, emphasis added).

Much of the time and energy and money we have put into developing our incredible church campuses and program offerings should have gone into improving our communities. A culture with rising poverty and illiteracy, disintegrating families and communities, declining morality, and diminishing economic opportunity will not sustain the church over the long run. The proof is right before our eyes.

It makes absolutely no sense—in fact, it's offensive—for congregations to promote multimillion-dollar building programs in cities where most kids in the public schools are on free or reduced lunch. Do we expect our state-of-the-art facilities to be received as good news by the people of those cities? And we wonder why people have a growing lack of respect for the church.

It is time for an about-face. I'm not suggesting that we tear down our church buildings, neglect to maintain our facilities, cut out all church building projects, or abandon all church programming. I am suggesting that we recalibrate our efforts and resources to reinvest in the welfare of our towns, cities, and neighborhoods. We should be developing microeconomic incubators for creating jobs, tutoring kids, beautifying our communities, planting community gardens on our church property and on abandoned lots, and opening medical clinics for the poor—and that's just for starters. Instead of hiring more church program developers and administrators to operate activities for church club members, we should hire community development staff.

I know of a growing number of church leaders who are doing all these things—and more—to invest in the communities where they are located. For instance, I recently spoke with Mark DeYmaz, who leads Mosaic Church of Central Arkansas, a "multiethnic and economically diverse" urban congregation in Little Rock. Mark and his congregation are a remarkable example of what I'm talking about.

- They consider their zip code in downtown Little Rock, which has the highest crime rate in the city, as their mission field.

- The congregation provides food to 52 percent of the zip code's population: 18,500 people each month.

- More than three hundred people are receiving free immigration legal service.

- Twenty young people who have aged out of the state's foster care system are being housed and mentored in four homes located on the church's property.

- In conjunction with Habitat for Humanity, the congregation is renovating six trailers to house more than forty women being rescued from drugs and prostitution.

- Since the church was first established in 2001, crime has dropped by ten percent within a one-mile radius of their facilities.

- Over $350,000 of economic impact was made last year alone through more than fifteen thousand hours of volunteer service by almost nine hundred people (more than twice the number of people attending Sunday services).

- More than sixty new jobs have been created as
the church has repurposed 180,000 square feet of
shuttered space to house its own ministry as well
as helping to establish 90,000 square feet of new
business retail space.

Mark is not in the church-building business. He is in the Kingdom business. He picked the roughest part of town to demonstrate what can happen when the church engages with the Kingdom agenda in the world. Mark believes that community transformation (Kingdom stuff) happens only when we pay attention to people's spiritual, social, and financial conditions. From his perspective, all three arenas must be part of the gospel ministry—bringing the good news of the Kingdom to bear on earth as it is in heaven.

Kingdom Coordinates

Seeking and pursuing the mission of the Kingdom are first and foremost in a Kingdom-centered approach to the church's ministry. We must have a narrative framework that supports this fundamental truth.

For the past five hundred years of the denominational era (which was birthed by the Reformation), the church-centered storyline has focused on separating church players based on theological systems (e.g., recognized spiritual gifts, mode of observing the sacraments, who is authorized to do what). Not only has this proven bewildering to nonchurch people, but it has also diminished the capacity of the body of Christ to collaborate in seeking "the peace and prosperity of the city."

The Kingdom saga, when it catches on, replaces this isolation and competition with new ways of collaboration. When this happens, the floodgates of blessing are opened to promote the life of the community. When the social capital bundled up in the church is unbundled for Kingdom priorities and Kingdom work, the Kingdom advances and the King is glorified.

I received an e-mail the other day detailing the story of how a prayer ministry of pastors in a Midwestern city has given birth to a multi-congregational, multi-denominational school-adoption initiative. Thousands of schoolchildren are now getting all kinds of help—from school supplies to homework buddies to reading coaches to weekend food packs—because churches are learning to play together in the Kingdom arena.

Living out the mission of the Kingdom must accompany or at times even precede our preaching of the message of the Kingdom. A friend of mine puts it like this: *Demonstration* now trumps *proclamation* as a way of securing a hearing for the gospel. Jesus did both. His good deeds and miracles piqued people's interest as well as authenticated his spiritual authority. The early movement of Jesus-followers continued his dynamic of *demonstrating* the Kingdom, especially through sacrificial service to their neighbors. But before long the church became institutionalized, and Christendom patterned itself after the ways of earthly kingdoms, creating noblemen (clergy), castles (cathedrals), and taxes (tithes and offerings claimed exclusively for "church work").

The collapse of the Christendom worldview makes it imperative that the church regain the Kingdom narrative that propelled the Christian movement in the pre-Christendom era. By living lives that improve others' lives, the people of God live out the mission of the Kingdom. When we do this in a spirit of joy and celebration, we reflect the culture of the Kingdom and manifest the Kingdom of Heaven here on earth.

One of my clients leads a congregation that routinely hosts block parties for the neighborhood surrounding the church—a neighborhood in transition. They are always working to find new games for the neighborhood kids, new food offerings they can serve, new ways to provide fun for the people in their most immediate sphere of influence. When I was with this pastor recently, he told me about a conversation he'd had with a newcomer at one of their parties.

"Who are you people?" the new neighbor asked. "And why are you doing this?"

The pastor, a wonderful Kingdom ambassador, represented the King well with his answers. He explained to the inquirer that helping people to enjoy life a little more, providing safe and wholesome entertainment for kids and for families, was one way the congregation wanted to serve the community. That Kingdom spirit and approach ensured that this wouldn't be the last time these two men would talk.

The people of God are free to work with anyone who is working for the Kingdom agenda. In our workshops, we sometimes show a picture of a community rally organized to show support for people afflicted with AIDS. In the picture, placards from two organizations are hoisted side by side. One placard displays the name of a well-known evangelical congregation. The other placard carries the logo of Planned

Parenthood of America. We can readily acknowledge that these two groups have little in common by way of values or agenda; yet at this event they joined together—along with many other groups—to promote a cause that both groups could support.

This type of intersection sets up a Kingdom scenario—two groups of people, only one of which is faith based and faith motivated, working together to help people experience a better quality of life. Imagine the possibilities for conversation and for a fresh appreciation of what each group brings to the table. Hopefully, part of that day's experience involved the development of some new respect, at least, and possibly some new relationships that can break down prejudice and judgmental attitudes in both groups.

Kingdom people can afford to be inclusive like this, because the Kingdom is not at risk. We understand that our covenant (going back to Abraham) is to bless everybody. It's not our job to decide who gets God's blessings. This perspective grants us the freedom to live, love, and serve with no strings attached. When we represent the Kingdom, we're free to bless people. I like the way Billy Graham said it: "It is God's job to judge, the Spirit's job to convict, and my job to love."[1]

How groups see themselves creates the reality in which they operate. Of particular interest for our discussion is the difference between groups that see themselves as *bounded sets* versus those that operate as *centered sets*, a distinction noted by sociologist Paul Hiebert.[2] Bounded-set groups organize around a shared set of beliefs and values that are used as a "boundary" to determine who is *in* or *out* of the group. Only those who subscribe to the membership doctrine are considered insiders. This is how the church-centered narrative has often been expressed: who's in and who's out. Hand in glove with this perspective is the idea that working with "outsiders" (even other church groups with different boundaries) violates the group norm.

A centered-set perspective, on the other hand, is defined by *relationship* and *direction* relative to a center point. Those moving toward the center are considered part of the set, whereas those who are moving away from the center are not. A centered-set Kingdom mentality places the Kingdom at the center and allows people to find themselves in relation to the center, moving either toward or away from life as God intends it.

When we reflect on Jesus' call to discipleship, we remember that it was an invitation to choose a direction—"follow me"—and not a command to adopt a doctrinal manifesto or align with a set of religious rites. There are people in the world outside of the church who are moving at great speed toward God's work in the world, whether they (or we) realize it or not. Likewise, there are people who associate themselves with the church but who are rushing away from the Kingdom—again, whether they realize it or not.

The church-centered narrative has drawn the circle tighter and tighter around who can be included as "us." The result has been to convince the world that the church is full of hypocrisy, prejudice, judgment, and condescension toward the rest of the culture. I think it's time for another storyline: "God wants something better for the lives of the people in our community. We want to help. You want to help. Let's do this together!"

We still need leaders and programming for the church, but the agenda must become more Kingdom-informed. Almost every time I speak, someone asks the question: "What is the role of pastors in this Kingdom emphasis?" Often someone will also ask, "How does this shift affect church programming?" (Usually they mention worship specifically.) These are appropriate questions. If leadership behavior and focus don't change, there's little hope that the church-as-institution can make this shift.

In the chapters ahead, we'll look more closely at leadership behaviors and strategies, but let me say this for now: The church still needs leaders, including those mentioned in Ephesians 4—apostles, prophets, evangelists, pastors, and teachers. These leaders do not all have to be clergy; in the New Testament context, these roles were not "church jobs." God's people still need teaching, pastoral care, reminders of their mission and identity in the world, and encouragement in introducing their friends and neighbors to Jesus. We still need to worship God and support others in their service to the King around the world.

However, church leaders whose priority is to build the church are not functioning in proper alignment with the mission of God. Church activities that function primarily to keep club members occupied violate the proper work that spiritual leaders should be engaged in. Church leaders must exhibit courage and vision in order to reorient their roles and functions around a Kingdom perspective. When the people of God are served and equipped by Kingdom-minded leaders, they learn how to partner with God (and with one another) in his redemptive mission in the world. This understanding of the role and responsibility of Kingdom-centered leadership will influence how we gather; how we worship; how and what we teach; and how we determine the emphasis, scope, and tone of church programming.

If churches want to move toward a Kingdom-centered narrative, we must speak up about a broader range of issues. I'm not talking about more sermons on more topics, or more declarations and resolutions issued by church groups. I mean actually addressing big societal issues, working to move the needle on quality-of-life issues like health care, literacy, job creation, hunger, institutional and generational poverty, racism, and the environment, to name some of the obvious ones. We can no longer pass by on the other side of the street like the two religious leaders in Jesus' story of the Good Samaritan. We have to get off our high horse (or donkey, in the case of the Samaritan) and help somebody.

You may think that these points are obvious enough for everyone to grasp and that there's no need to drum it in. All I can say is that, in my work with church leaders and congregations, I still battle a disappointing lack of response to the pressing needs all around us. Some of it is driven by fear or a sense that we can't make a difference. More often, the lack of action results from being too busy with religious stuff or from flat-out apathy to the needs of others.

I had lunch not long ago with a prominent church leader to discuss his participation in a local, multi-congregational community service initiative. "I'm very interested in what you're doing," he said, "but right now I just can't add anything else to my plate." What was on his plate? A capital stewardship campaign for church renovation, a writing project, a church staff search, and developing the fall worship themes and experiences. All church stuff. To him, it made perfect sense to be so consumed by his church-centered universe that he had no time for a greater Kingdom agenda.

A few summers ago, my family and I visited the Mauthausen concentration camp on the banks of the Danube River between Salzburg and Vienna in Austria. Almost 200,000 people were brought to this facility between 1938 and 1945. Half of them—100,000 people—died in the gas chamber or from starvation, mistreatment, or illness. My older daughter's question as we toured the memorial still haunts me: "Daddy, isn't Austria a Christian country?" I knew exactly what prompted her question. There was no way that the people of Mauthausen could not have known what was happening on the hill overlooking their village, especially since the deportees were unloaded at the train station in the center of town. Though there were many acts of courage by people under Nazi subjugation to help the poor souls in this camp, the truth is that church services went on unabated while people were dying by the thousands.

In my office, I keep the brochure I picked up at the memorial close by. It forces me to ask the question, "What's going on right now in our own village?" while we increase our schedule of church services, build our buildings, enjoy our church chef's cuisine (yes, some churches have chefs), plan our ski trips, and get together as church leaders to figure out how we can do all this better. It's easy, in retrospect, to judge the people of Mauthausen, but what church games are *we* playing while people in our cities and towns are suffering in captivity to sin, sickness, poverty, and injustice?

We Have a Story to Tell to the Nations

Jesus did not establish the church to start a new religion called Christianity. He established the church as an expression of the Kingdom for the people of God as they partner with him in his redemptive mission in the world.

God's mission in the world has not changed. But in much of the church today, the idea of serving God has morphed into "becoming a good church member." People are considered disciples based on their faithful support of and participation in church activities, not necessarily on whether they are growing toward or reflecting the heart of Jesus for others and the world.

In short, turning people into good church people has largely become the mission of the church. It promotes and perpetuates a church-centered narrative. But just as he did with religious leaders in his own day, Jesus has a beef with church leaders who misrepresent God to the world, who are telling the wrong story.

The story that the church tells must change. I'm not just talking about *how* the story is told—a concern that has given rise to all the church "fixes" of my lifetime, including the seeker-sensitive, cultural-relevance, contemporary-worship, church-growth, emerging-church, and church-health movements—I'm talking about the *content* of the story. The church can no longer posture itself as the star of the show or even as the primary platform where the story unfolds. Church-centeredness must give way to the fullness of the Kingdom saga.

The Kingdom is the show. The King is the star. Life is the plot. This is the story that interests everyone, because they are involved in it.

5

AIDING AND ABETTING
THE KINGDOM

A GROUP OF CHURCH LEADERS who had convened to consider
a literacy initiative in their city invited me to help with some
collaborative strategies. During the discussion, one of the
youth pastors expressed his reservations with the project.

"I just don't think it's the church's job to teach kids to read."

His declaration, which reflected an ignorance of the history of the church's role in education, left me slack-jawed.
After all, Sunday school was originally a literacy campaign
for kids on the streets of London. Many of the earliest
colleges on American soil—including Harvard, Yale, and
Princeton—were church-sponsored centers of higher education. But more to the point of our discussion, this young
man's perspective illustrates the need for the church to understand its Kingdom mandate.

Nothing short of a re-theologizing will help us recapture the Kingdom narrative. And given how entrenched the church-centered story has become, it's probably not going to be easy.

The ecclesiological fervor of the past five hundred years has supported the development of a church-centered narrative, in North America in particular. Ever since Luther tacked up his ninety-five theses, the church has been consumed with "proper doctrine." In recent centuries, theological discussions have focused primarily on church issues and related themes: what constitutes a New Testament church; who is authorized to do what in a church setting; how the gifts of the Spirit operate in church life; how someone gains entrance to the church and remains in good standing; which forms of polity best serve the church's leadership needs—the list goes on and on. How different groups resolved these various issues of doctrine and structure became recognizable distinctions between church tribes. Thousands of denominations, associations, and networks have developed over the past several hundred years, each distinguished by their particular recipe for "doing church."

A Kingdom-centered narrative, on the other hand, focuses on how to *be* the church in the world, and the issues for Kingdom agents are fundamentally different from those that concern leaders and managers of institutional churches. Missional Jesus-followers are not obsessed with *how* or *where* they worship or *who* is authorized to do *what* in church gatherings.

Their spiritual journey is not defined by the form of church they attend. They are found in every tribe. Some attend cathedrals, while others participate in program-heavy evangelical congregations and still others gather in homes. Whether they are stay-at-home moms or executives of multinational corporations, their focus is on creating greater missional intentionality in every part of their lives—where they live, work, go to school, and play.

This effort can involve everything from drastically reorienting life priorities to looking for ways to create greater personal margins of time, money, and energy so they can serve as effective Kingdom agents. People living out a Kingdom-focused narrative don't see life as being compartmentalized into sacred or secular components. For them, every activity and relationship is an opportunity to be a person of blessing, to help people know God and enjoy the life he wants for them. The neighborhood book club, the boardroom, the office, the schoolroom, the gym, and the sanctuary in a church building—all are places for God encounters. Kingdom people look for God at work in the world and are open to how they can partner with his work that is already underway in the people they meet and the encounters they have.

This way of life reflects the biblical narrative about God's mission on earth. It is a story that has been with us all along from the beginning of human history, before the rise of the church-centered focus fostered by Christendom.

This chapter aims to shine a light on key topics for theological development that are both supportive of and profoundly affected by a Kingdom narrative. These items fall into three broad categories: God's mission, church expression, and personal Kingdom engagement. Students of systematic theology will likely notice that this treatment does not reflect the classic categories involved in a comprehensive theological system. Our goal here is to start a conversation, not to have the last word. Other leaders and thinkers have already joined the discussion. Many more will add their voices in the days to come. It will take a bunch of us, working and writing from various angles, to move the prevailing theological focus from the church to the Kingdom.

God's Mission (*Missio Dei*)

God is on a mission. This fact was made plain from the very beginning in the Garden of Eden. God initiated the search for Adam to reengage with him after the Fall. God came looking for Adam—not because he didn't know where Adam was but because he was determined that the entrance of sin into the world would not destroy his relationship with humanity.

As we know, when God showed up in the Garden post-Fall, it was not without a plan. He announced judgment and the means of restoration all at once. He dealt with the immediate devastation while setting in motion the elements of redemption.

We have well established that God's mission centers on his Kingdom. The Kingdom saga runs from Genesis to Revelation, from the first moment of created time into eternity. God's pursuit of his mission transcends artificial human boundaries of nationality, life cycles, rulers, and religion. God alone owns his mission; he does not need our help with it, and he is never at risk of failure. His mission may, in fact, have another chapter to it beyond the earthbound story spelled out in biblical literature. But for now we can affirm that God's mission of granting life as he intends it focuses squarely on the earth. Jesus taught us to pray for the Kingdom to come on *earth* as it is in heaven. The Kingdom saga is playing out in time and space. It is the central story of all human history.

God himself entered into time and space in the person of Jesus: a miraculous, mysterious, and unique incarnation. The Son of God played an unanticipated (by humans) role in the Kingdom saga through his unimaginable sacrifice, beginning with his leaving heaven to enter into this world at Bethlehem.

Jesus came on the public scene, announcing the good news (gospel) of the Kingdom. His miracles demonstrated the power and purpose of the Kingdom. Jesus' life displayed the attributes of the Kingdom. His invasion of Satan's stronghold to break the hold of sin, death, and the grave revealed the depth of God's determination that we could experience life as he always intended. Jesus did not sacrifice himself because "God so loved the church." As he told Nicodemus, he came because God "so loved the *world*." The world is the target of God's redemptive mission.

When Jesus ascended back to the Father, it opened the way for the coming of the Spirit he had promised to send. The Holy Spirit birthed the church and gave—*gives*—it the power to fulfill its role in the Kingdom saga. The same Spirit who animated and energized Jesus in the flesh creates and facilitates the ongoing presence of Jesus in the lives of his followers. The Kingdom life of Jesus flows through those who are connected to him, as branches receive life from the vine. The fruit of Jesus' Kingdom life is a continuing Kingdom life in his disciples, a reality made possible through the ministry of the Holy Spirit. This is why Jesus prophesied that his followers would continue his works as contemporary examples of the Kingdom.

Church Expression

In a church-centered worldview, we confuse what the church does when it gathers—its worship, practice of sacraments, and teaching—as the core of its identity and role. These are not the identity of the church, any more than a haircut or wardrobe conveys the essence of a person's identity.

A Kingdom-oriented ecclesiology focuses on the work of the church *in the world*, because that mission expresses our identity and role. The biblical witness reveals that church is a relationship. We are the people of God—in active, vital relationship with him and with one another. By God's covenant with Abraham in Genesis 12:1-2, we are people of blessing, created to bless the world as a way of embodying the mission of God so that people can understand who he is and can connect with life as he intends it. This is who we are; this is our identity, 24/7/365. There is never a time when we are not the church. Every action, conversation, and decision is informed by and plays out against the backdrop of the relationship we have with Jesus. Everywhere I go, everywhere you go, there the church is.

The church was created on purpose, *for* a purpose—to partner with God in his redemptive mission here on earth. The biblical record portrays this role through a powerful image: a kingdom of priests. That's how we are to function.

The Priesthood of All Believers

The designation of God's people as a kingdom of priests was first disclosed to Moses during his momentous meeting with God on Mount Sinai after the Exodus. In Moses' earlier encounter with God on this same mountain (in the episode with the burning bush), God had instructed him to come back to that spot, bringing God's people with him (Exodus 3:12). Imagine the eagerness and anticipation that accompanied Moses on his ascent to meet with God on the mountain, to find out his next instructions. This time, the directives Moses received were not just for him, but also for the rescued slaves.

> Then Moses climbed the mountain to appear before God. The LORD called to him from the mountain and said, "Give these instructions to the family of Jacob; announce it to the descendants of Israel: 'You have seen what I did to the Egyptians. You know how I carried you on eagles' wings and brought you to myself. Now if you will obey me and keep my covenant, you will be my own special treasure from among all the peoples on earth; for all the earth belongs to me. And you will be my kingdom of priests, my holy nation.' This is the message you must give to the people of Israel."
> (Exodus 19:3-6)

This significant directive—giving further definition to the Abrahamic covenant—revealed that Israel had the responsibility to act as God's priests *to* and *in* the world. The Old Testament chronicles the tension and struggle as Israel wrestled with this mandate. Though the Aaronic priesthood was instituted by God, over time it fostered a religion based on rite observance, which inadequately reflected God's heart. (This was Jesus' criticism of the institutional Judaism of his day.) The Old Testament prophets repeatedly addressed the missional drift of the nation, reminding Israel of their calling to be priests to the world.

The transition from the Old Testament to the New Testament did not change this calling. Peter and John borrow both concept and language from Exodus 19 in their explicit statements regarding our role as the church.

> You are living stones that God is building into his spiritual temple. What's more, you are his holy priests. Through the mediation of Jesus Christ, you offer spiritual sacrifices that please God. . . . For you are a chosen people. You are royal priests, a holy nation, God's very own possession. As a result, you can show others the goodness of God, for he called you out of the darkness into his wonderful light. (1 Peter 2:5, 9)

In Revelation 1:6, John begins his message to the churches by reminding them of the result of Christ's work in them: "He has made us a Kingdom of priests for God his Father." Later in Revelation, in the apostle's description of a worship experience in heaven, the elders and creatures around the throne break into a song of praise to the Lamb:

They sang a new song with these words: "You are worthy to take the scroll and break its seals and open it. For you were slaughtered, and your blood has ransomed people for God from every tribe and language and people and nation. And you have caused them to become a Kingdom of priests for our God." (Revelation 5:9-10)

Note that the role reserved for Israel in the Old Testament is now extended to every ransomed person, regardless of background. The entire church inherits the call.

Between the Old Testament and the New Testament, we see the progression of this doctrine from *promise* to *realization*. In Exodus 19, God's promise to Moses (you *will be* my kingdom of priests) signals the commencement of a status that will play out into the future. In Revelation, John indicates an already completed action (you *have caused them to become*). Peter's use of the present tense (you *are* royal priests) highlights our ongoing role in the present age.

The doctrine of the priesthood of all believers—a teaching espoused throughout the Bible—expresses both the identity and role of the church.

Some Kingdom Implications

During the Reformation, Martin Luther called attention to the biblical doctrine of the priesthood of all believers. He saw the teaching as fundamental to Christian vocation in the world. For Luther and others, it also strengthened the argument against the clerical hierarchy of Rome.

In our day, the doctrine offers far more than a polemical

argument in a clash of church methodologies. It establishes a basis for a fundamental shift in our understanding of how the church shows up in the world. A proper application of this biblical teaching moves the center of gravity for God's mission toward an ecclesiology built on people (their passion and gifts) rather than on institutional structures and systems. It taps into a metaphor repeated throughout the Bible that helps us apprehend how we engage with and participate in the mission of God. In short, it gives us a way to transition the narrative of the body of Christ away from a church-centered story to a focus on the Kingdom saga.

Here are some of the implications of this underapplied biblical theme. They are grouped broadly under "corporate expression" and "personal engagement."

Corporate Expression

The doctrine of the universal priesthood of believers provides a theological underpinning for moving from a church-centered narrative to a Kingdom-centered narrative.

Church is a *who*, not a *what*, because the church embodies a relationship between God and a people, not between him and a thing, a place, or a set of practices. Places and practices may serve the relationship—just as my wife and I have a home and do certain things as a married couple—but they do not define the relationship.

We need to expand our understanding of how the church expresses itself. The familiar congregational forms will continue to serve millions of people, but they are being joined by other forms of church life in North America. We're already familiar with house churches, missional communities,

Internet campuses, and a revival of monastic orders, but we have not yet seen all of the forms of church expression that will emerge as Jesus-followers seek to fulfill their mission as priests in the world. The mode of church does not define the church's core identity. Mode supports mission, not the other way around.

In order for every crack and crevice of our culture to be exposed to the gospel of the Kingdom, the church will increasingly manifest itself outside the walls of the traditional, institutional organization. While I was in Great Britain recently, I had a conversation with a Welsh pastor and his wife, who had "planted the church" in a coffee shop they opened in the small town where they live.

"The townspeople say they encounter something 'very different' in our shop," the wife told me. "Some people just burst into tears ordering coffee, saying they don't know why exactly, except for an overwhelming sense of peace. Of course, *we* know they are encountering the Holy Spirit. It gives us many opportunities to open up spiritual dialogue."

Their shop has revitalized a part of the town center, creating jobs and enhancing community life. Their reputation has grown to the point that three local public schools have asked them to "plant the church" on their campuses.

In a church-centered paradigm, the laity are largely expected to cheer on the clergy, admire their gifts, and help them accomplish church programming. In a Kingdom-centered paradigm, the clergy cheer on and support the laity, who are seen as the primary agents of the church's work in the world.

Here's an example of what I mean. A pastor related to

me the story of an older Boomer in his congregation who said he had been "wrecked by God" through a new faith adventure. Newly retired, the man felt God's call to engage the club culture in his community. Nothing about the clubs appealed to him, yet he felt *sent* to this environment. He just started going and hanging out one night a week from about 10 p.m. until 4 a.m.

"I don't know what I'm doing, except just being available to people for conversation," he said to the pastor on more than one occasion.

Apparently, God knows what he is doing. Young men are drawn to this guy like a magnet. Over the past few months, he has engaged so many in spiritual conversation that several dozen are now meeting weekly for Bible study and prayer.

"What am I supposed to do for this man?" the pastor asked me.

"What are you doing *now*?"

"I pray for him, ask him how things are going, speak into some of the club conversations he brings to me for advice, and let him tell his story to others in our congregation."

"Perfect!" I replied. "You don't need to do anything else."

This pastor has it exactly right—he's equipping this club-culture priest for the work of the ministry.

Worship gatherings may be affected in several ways. First, if we recognize more priests, more priests will probably be involved in the various things that go on. In the current, clergy-centric system, the clear message communicated in our "worship services" is that the church really belongs to a select few. But other than tradition and clergy-controlled educational credentialing, there is really no good reason why wisdom and insight from a greater number of people can't be shared, and why people not wearing collars and robes can't preside over liturgical rites. Such a "democratization" would not spell the end of leadership; it would broaden it.

The *content* of our gatherings would also shift. More attention would be focused on what happens between gatherings. In addition to worship and biblical teaching, we would hear more about God's work in *all* domains (families, neighborhoods, schools, businesses, etc.). We would become more intentional about acquainting *everyone* with needs and opportunities for service, in order to better love our neighbors and fulfill one of the greatest commandments (Matthew 22:36-40). More emphasis would be placed on incarnational expressions of Jesus-following rather than on creating "a great worship experience" for pew-bound consumers. Fresh, local, and immediate stories of God's transforming power in people's lives—both to turn around desperate situations and to meet everyday needs—would add greater depth and dimension to our worship. Our sense of awe and reverence for God would grow, even as we reveled in his marvelous acts.

Church programming would focus on *developing* and *deploying* missional Jesus-followers, compassionate believer-priests who are equipped to serve as Kingdom agents in whatever settings the King has assigned them in life. Local mission experiences would increase dramatically as believer-priests sought for ways to bless their cities and neighborhoods.

Educational ministries would focus on enriching the work in the world of these deployed priests, rather than endlessly teaching principles and hoping that they will somehow be translated into application.

Intergenerational sharing would either augment or replace the traditional, age-segregated classroom approach. Children's and student ministries would become more relationally focused and mentor-driven, rather than entertainment-centered. Parents would be equipped and encouraged to have conversations about God with their children in order to help them navigate a culture increasingly less supportive of traditional Christian values and behaviors.

A person's development path would be less scripted ("show up and we'll take it from here"—the program-driven approach) and more customized and coached. Teens, for example, might be involved in mentoring teams focused on their personal and spiritual development; and they might have multiple mentors, including a grandparent figure, a parent peer, and a young adult they respect.

Staff assignments would shift from focusing on project management to training and equipping coaches and mentors, as well as developing community relationships for greater strategic missional engagement.

Women's and men's ministries would no longer be characterized only by teaching and fellowship but also by service projects targeting gender-specific issues or places where gender-specific involvement is advantageous (such as prison ministry or abuse shelters).

Church websites would become resource rich and would focus more on life development than on simply serving as congregational bulletin boards for church-related activities. They would also integrate service opportunities inside and outside the church, so that, for example, people interested in children's ministries would be able to explore on the same page opportunities for service in church child care and at the local elementary school.

We must broaden our understanding of the gifts listed in Ephesians 4:11 (apostles, prophets, evangelists, pastors, teachers) that Christ gave to the church. In the church-centric congregational era, these gifts have become largely professionalized jobs and offices. A renewed Kingdom awareness will allow the gifts to be unshackled from the institutional church culture to permeate the world at large. After all, these are gifts wrapped inside people who are naturally dispersed into the culture by the simple virtue of living their lives.

In the distributed church of the universal priesthood, these gifted people operate in every sector of society. *Apostolic* Jesus-followers explore and employ new methods of gospel expression. They serve as missional strategists to help the church embrace its role in the world and devise ways of sharing the good news of the Kingdom.

The *prophetic* element involves speaking truth into people's lives with particular accuracy and spiritual insight. The prophetic gift sees the need behind the need in order to get to real issues. These insights and admonitions can be delivered in individual settings (such as a counseling session) or may take a more public path by calling attention to societal ills or the cause of justice (much as the Old Testaments prophets did). Modern-day prophets may encourage people to start organizations that deal with social issues or to form businesses that create jobs and revitalize neighborhoods.

By sharing their faith in their spheres of influence (in neighborhoods, businesses, classrooms, sports organizations, the medical field, etc.), the *evangelists* open up spiritual dialogues. Many of these opportunities will be uncovered or created as God's people adopt a servant posture. Being ready to give an answer for the hope within them, evangelists are adept at helping people appropriate for themselves the redemptive work of Jesus. They also help others to learn how to shape similar conversations.

In a Kingdom paradigm, there remains a vital role for traditional, professional *pastors* who function in traditional, institutional church roles. But not all pastors will continue to exercise their gifts in typical church settings.

I received an e-mail the other day that started like this: "You don't know me. I'm a Christ-follower who has served him as a pastor for twenty-five years. I'm in the process of transitioning into a corporate pastor-type role in a local business." We will see more examples like this as the link between the Kingdom narrative and the universal priesthood grows stronger. We will also celebrate business leaders, educators, physicians, sanitation workers, journalists, and people in every human endeavor who exercise a decidedly pastoral nature in how they deal with people in their respective domains.

Finally, the church has a need for *teachers* who can equip the dispersed saints to serve as Kingdom agents. Not all this teaching will take place inside church classrooms or auditoriums. Facebook, the blogosphere, the Twittersphere, podcasts, YouTube—these terms weren't even words twenty years ago, much less real spaces made possible by the digital information revolution. All these arenas, and others that have yet to be devised, provide opportunities for teachers to share spiritual insight for Kingdom living.

When the church of faithful, Jesus-following priests

partners with God in his Kingdom mission, we can expect to see a positive impact on quality-of-life indexes in our communities: job creation going up; crime rates going down; and literacy, health care, and family life all improving as Kingdom priests devote themselves to making a difference in these and other issues that ignite their passions and break their hearts.

A young Jesus-follower and businessman I met in England shared with me part of his intriguing story. As he put it, God has "given him favor" by positioning him as the primary confidant and advisor to a billionaire investor who plans to open hundreds of nursing-care facilities for the aging population in China. This advisor, himself of Chinese descent, believes that this opportunity is his platform not only to take care of people but also to spread the salt and light of the gospel across China.

Personal Kingdom Engagement

I remember having dinner with a friend who is an accomplished attorney. As a student, he was tops in his law class, and today he has achieved the rank of senior partner in a very large law firm. Teams of lawyers in three states report to him. He is also a follower of Jesus, tops in his class as a churchman.

My friend has held every lay leader position in his congregation and is esteemed as a mature Christian by everyone who knows him. The problem is that he has never figured out how to personally engage with the mission of God.

"I know that my law practice is supposed to be my mission field," he told me, "but I have no idea how to do that." The church-centered discipleship model he grew up under has produced a world-class church leader but a missionally challenged Jesus-follower, deployed in the world but not adequately equipped.

Sadly, he is not alone. My friend is but one example of millions of other gifted and passionate people who are bundled up at church, investing time, talent, and treasure in perpetuating the church's programs, all the while waiting and yearning (whether they realize it or not) to be unleashed on the world as viral Kingdom agents.

This situation will be set right only when a Kingdom perspective becomes more important than teaching people to "serve God by serving the church." Returning for a moment to the centered-set example mentioned in chapter 4, as we move in the direction of our relationship with Jesus Christ (our center), we align ourselves with his Kingdom mission and follow him out into the world to serve people and promote life as God intends it.

As we (the church) follow after Jesus as deployed agents of the Kingdom, our renewed focus will result in a shift in the assumptions, methods, and goals of our discipleship. The following items are a few examples of what I mean.

1. We must broaden our concept of discipleship. Although in most church settings discipleship is seen as an activity for believers, a Kingdom orientation begins with people wherever they are on the belief continuum, often even before they know who Jesus is. A coffee shop owner told me recently that she had struck up a relationship with a patron who had lost her job due to carpal tunnel syndrome. After months of praying for this woman and encouraging her, the shop owner hired her as a baker.

"She's not a Jesus-follower—yet," the owner said with a

twinkle in her eye. If the Kingdom agenda is about life as God intends it, anything we do to help people experience this life qualifies as some measure of disciple-making. Any effort that improves people's capacity to be better parents, better workers, or better neighbors constitutes a discipleship effort—as long the goal is to help people experience life as God intends it. Helping people *become* people (by removing obstacles that prevented them from living life as God intends it—through healings, resurrections, casting out demons, and pulling people out of bad situations) seemed to be Jesus' goal, and he invites you and me to follow in his footsteps. Discipleship is people development.

2. Serving others must become a more intentional spiritual discipline. Whereas church-centered discipleship has tended to focus on acquisition of information (Bible knowledge) and engagement in personalized spiritual activity (worship, prayer, and study), a Kingdom discipleship agenda will prioritize transformational living, which assumes that loving God and loving our neighbors are bedrock principles of spiritual formation. Jesus went into the world and modeled this two-pronged love. And then he said, "Now go and *do* the same" (Luke 10:37, emphasis added).

Helping others provides a wonderful path toward our own self-awareness. When serving others in need, we become more aware of ourselves—our biases, prejudices, boundaries, and presuppositions about others. This awareness involves the development of empathy, a sense of responsibility, and compassion for the needy. All these characteristics involve behavioral and attitudinal shifts, which is the hard part of disciple-making.

3. We need to pay more attention to Ephesians 2:10. So much emphasis, especially in evangelical circles, has been showered on Ephesians 2:8-9: "God saved you by his grace when you believed. And you can't take credit for this: it is a gift from God. Salvation is not a reward for the good things we have done, so none of us can boast about it." When we stop there, without including verse 10, we truncate the full flow and meaning of the text. We need verse 10 to complete the thought: "For we are God's masterpiece. He has created us anew in Christ Jesus, so we can do the good things he planned for us long ago."

We were not just saved *from* our sins *through* the work of Jesus on the cross; we were also saved *to do* something. And that something is very specific: good works that God planned for us ahead of time. These "good works" are an essential component of our development as disciples. If we don't do them, we are lesser disciples than we would be otherwise. A major role of discipleship, then, is to help people figure out what these works are and how to pursue them in their lives.

4. Our training of pastors must focus on helping them become disciple-makers. My seminary training was conducted under the oft-cited paradigm that our job was to equip the people of God to do the work of ministry (Ephesians 4:12). The problem was that, in our church-centered thinking, we reduced the "work of ministry" down to church work. It never occurred to me that the "work of ministry," at the time that Ephesians was written, occurred primarily in the marketplace. A Kingdom emphasis means that my job as a pastor and teacher is to help people know how to minister when they're away from worship services, church programs, and church real estate. However, not a single seminary course I took taught me how to do this. All of my studies helped me to become a better leader and manager of the church as an institution but not of the church as *people*, as deployed agents of the Kingdom.

5. The focus of leadership must shift from "meeting budget" to developing generous people. In the church-centered narrative I grew up in, supported by centuries of teaching and practice, one's giving was expected to be directed to the church. Even those pastors and teachers who countenanced charitable giving to organizations and efforts outside the church said that this should be practiced only after the tithe was given to the church coffers. I preached these views myself, contending forcefully that the Old Testament practice of storehouse tithing had transferred to the New Testament as one's obligation to give gifts to the church. I thought I had all kinds of scriptural support, including Jesus' pat on the back to the Pharisees for their tithing and his glowing affirmation of the widow who gave all she had to the treasure of the Temple. But I was wrong.

The Kingdom narrative celebrates people helping people—directly, out-of-pocket, not necessarily collected and administered by the church (though it may be done this way, as in Acts 4:35). Maybe this wouldn't be such an issue if more of the funds that the church receives were sown back into the community rather than being spent on mortgage payments, facilities maintenance, marketing, and payroll. Each year, more than $100 billion flows into the coffers of faith-based organizations in the United States alone. It's hard to reconcile that figure with the fact that one-sixth of Americans are food challenged or that school-aged kids lack shoes to wear to school, to cite just two of a number of disturbing realities in American society. I met a pastor at a conference who told me that his goal was for his congregation to keep only a tithe of what it received and to release 90 percent of its offerings into community ministry. May his tribe increase!

A Kingdom-centered narrative doesn't mean that people should stop supporting church program budgets. Not at all. But it does mean that the focus of tithing should shift away from maintaining the church budget and toward helping the needy. Generous people will support what is important to them, including the church budget. In addition, other sources of revenue beyond member giving are increasingly available to congregations engaged in Kingdom agendas: foundations, grants, for-profit entrepreneurial ventures, and altruistic individuals who want to invest in something they're passionate about (such as education or health care). One organization I worked with received $250,000 from a generous individual to help fund church planting. He said, "I'm not a church person, but if you are serious about building a better community, I want to help." Once people become involved financially with the church, doors are opened for discipleship. As Jesus said, our hearts follow our treasure.

The topic of *vocation* becomes profoundly more important in a Kingdom-centered theology. A church-centered ecclesiology typically focuses on "the call" as exclusively related to church work, with scant attention paid to the work of God's people in their daily occupations.

"I resent it every time I hear pastors talk about their 'call' as something exclusive to their line of work," an attorney told me. "I feel every bit as called as they do to the work I'm doing." I have heard similar sentiments from moms, teachers, health-care workers, social workers, business leaders, not-for-profit organizational workers, and people who spend their time in public-sector jobs.

"God didn't make people to get work done," Don Clifton, the former chairman of Gallup, used to say. "He made work to get people done." This insightful understanding of the value of work explains why we are compelled in a Kingdom narrative to help people gain meaningful employment and to see their employment as meaningful.

Seeing the image of God in all people becomes a central element in how we relate to society from a Kingdom-based perspective. Every person bears God's image. It's part of what makes us human, separates us from the rest of creation, and connects us with each other and God.

A healthy appreciation for the image of God in people can help us repair the sin of "us versus them" that separates us from one another. It can keep us from dishonoring people in how we try to help them. Understanding our common bond as human beings can help frame our conversations with people who do not share our faith or worldview. If we see people of other faiths as the enemy—that is, as *them* and not *us*—we are much more likely to think of evangelism as a confrontation and success as "winning." However, if we view other people as fellow bearers of the divine image, we can connect with them on our mutual interest in life that we all have.

The search for abundant life will inevitably lead to Jesus because he is the Life. Is it truth they seek for their journey?

We can confidently encourage their search, because Jesus is the Truth. Is it love they're after? God is Love, and we can talk about how he shows it.

Grounding our evangelism in the truth that we are all created in the image of God prevents the marketing-and-sales approach that has proven problematic. The sales approach to sharing Jesus views people outside the faith in a functional and nonrelational way—as marks to be converted. That's why so many church people, when the topic turns to evangelism, get sweaty-palmed and anxious. In their minds, the idea of evangelism involves trying to sell a product to people who aren't interested in it. However, when we realize that God is already at work in people's lives and bringing out his image in them, we're free to simply help in this endeavor, treating other people as fellow image bearers and remaining open to spiritual conversation.

I offer these theological reflections as suggestions for how the plot will thicken as the Kingdom narrative develops. My prayer is that God will raise up faithful and articulate practitioners and thinkers who will provide biblical and theological guidance to support a Kingdom storyline for the North American church. My hunch is that they will come from incarnational leaders and Kingdom agents distributed across every domain of culture. Their lives and their influence will reflect what it means to be the people of God, blessing their communities and providing a resurrection of hope for life as God intends it.

Maybe you're one of these people!

WHEN IT WORKS: KINGDOM COLLABORATION

"TEST SCORES UP. Attendance up. Trips to the school nurse down." The audience at the banquet event I was about to address heard these encouraging words from Judy, the president of Titus County Cares (TCC), the sponsoring organization. The assembled group of more than three hundred people served as volunteers for TCC in Mount Pleasant, Texas. Many of them helped to pack up to three tons of food each week into as many as one thousand backpacks that food-challenged kids (the ones receiving free or subsidized lunches at school during the week) could take home from school over the weekend. The school district had just released the information that Judy shared with the crowd, directly attributing the improved statistics to the backpack program.

My assignment that night was to provide a message of inspiration and motivation for the volunteer force, but those encouraging numbers from the school district did most of the work for me! All that was left for me was to celebrate their accomplishments and challenge them to tackle even more projects together to improve the lives of the people in that region—which they continue to do.

Although TCC is a faith-based organization, the banquet crowd represented every sector of that northeast Texas community: business, health care, education, government, media, the arts, and the not-for-profit social sector. TCC's work extends far beyond the backpack program. Each week, the organization feeds hungry families, helps with emergency rent and utility bills, and distributes clothes. During the summer, they sponsor a summer reading program as part of a literacy initiative that is under development. TCC is a great example of community collaboration.[1]

The story behind TCC is of particular interest to our discussion. Founded in May 2005, the organization was formed through the intentional repurposing of a small, decades-old ministerial alliance among local pastors. Today, TCC has a full-time paid staff, a new ministry center and warehouse, hundreds of volunteers, and a board composed of significant community leaders; and it is funded not only through church and individual donations but also through grants from multiple corporate entities and private and public foundations. All of this started with the innovative thinking of a group of concerned church leaders numbering less than a half dozen.

TCC is changing the church narrative in Titus County into a Kingdom-centered story. They are doing this by pointing the way to a broader Kingdom agenda for anyone in town who wants to seek the welfare and prosperity of the city. But even more, they provide any individual there—whether a person of faith or not—a way to participate in the Kingdom saga. Even while unapologetically following Jesus (they offer prayer to every person they help), they have garnered the respect and participation of all sectors of their county.

On another occasion, I visited Mount Pleasant to work with TCC on developing a strategy for a significant literacy initiative they were undertaking. Part of my work was to interface with key community leaders to gain their input and support. TCC was able to convene the mayor, the county judge, the police and fire chiefs, the sheriff, the superintendent of education, several bankers, and a group of local pastors. In other words, they were able to host the party. Why? Because they had earned street cred by delivering real help, serving their way into the hearts of the people of Titus County, Texas.

Do you want to be part of an epic story like this—moving from a church-centered narrative to a Kingdom saga? The answer is probably *yes*, or you wouldn't be reading this book. Truth be told, I find this sentiment bubbling up all across the country. However, turning these hopes into realized, life-enhancing outcomes requires more than just goodwill. As with TCC's experience, it takes some very specific ingredients to turn wishes into concrete results.

Want to know what those ingredients are? Let's take a look.

Collective Impact

For the past several years, the Stanford Center on Philanthropy and Civil Society at Stanford University has been studying what they call *collective impact*. In my own work in communities, I've been using the term *cross-domain collaboration*. For me, both terms refer to the same thing: how a community creates collaborative efforts across multiple sectors (public, private, social) that are designed to move the needle on big societal issues. As we have seen, these problems—hunger, education, health care, job creation, and poverty—are Kingdom-agenda issues because they pose a challenge to life as God intends it, threatening to rob people of the abundant life that God wants for them.

The work of the Stanford research team has proven very helpful in providing a common language to identify the key ingredients involved in developing and implementing effective community collaborative initiatives. These elements also provide a developmental path for pursuing community projects.

Preconditions

In order for collective impact to work, the Stanford researchers concluded, three preconditions must exist.[2]

First, an *influential champion*—or group of champions—must put their weight behind the effort. These are people who command enough respect in the community to bring people to the table to discuss the issue and make plans. In the case of Titus County Cares, the champions were a coalition of high-profile, longtime community leaders.

In Redwood City, California (near San Francisco), a community-wide literacy initiative is now underway. This effort never would have gotten off the ground without the convening power of a city council member—a local champion—who believed it was possible to harness the collective resources of the community to tackle a growing problem. When I made my first trip there to interview city leaders, I was able to meet with the mayor, the city manager, the newspaper publisher, two school superintendents, the police chief, the leaders of various civic organizations and community foundations, and prominent church leaders. What made these high-level conversations possible? It certainly wasn't me. These people didn't know me from Adam's house cat. But they all knew and respected John, the city council member whose position gave him the clout to pull this crew together. He also happened to be a Jesus-follower with a Kingdom mentality.

A second precondition essential to effective collective impact is the presence and commitment of *adequate financial resources* for at least two or three years. Often these resources come from an initial donor or donor group who wants to address a particular project or passion. In the case of Redwood City, a philanthropist promised to fund two years of my work there in order to get the project rolling. The same thing happened in Pensacola, Florida, where three donors put up the funding (about $35,000) for the planning phase of two initiatives designed to address education and health-care issues. Other funding will be needed for implementation, but without the start-up money for an eighteen-month strategy planning phase, the players never would have come together and the community effort never would have materialized.

A third precondition for collective impact, according to the Stanford team, involves having a *sense of urgency* for change. This urgency includes both a significant awareness of the problem and the accompanying conviction that new approaches must be applied in search of a solution. The uncertainty around the advent of the Affordable Care Act (ACA), along with Florida's decision to opt out of the ACA's expanded Medicaid provisions, created the requisite urgency needed for Influence Pensacola, a 501(c)(3) community organization, to pull together the four regional hospitals in Pensacola for an unprecedented collaboration. They are now crafting a community case-management initiative that will dramatically improve the delivery of health care to an at-risk portion of their population.

From my own experience in working to build cross-domain collaborative communities, I would add two additional preconditions to what the Stanford team identified. I believe that groups who want to collaborate need a *conversation coach* who can shape the discussion. Even if a champion calls the meeting, money is in the bank, and everyone in the room is primed for action, the conversation can break down because no one really knows how to proceed. Without appropriate coaching on an intentional direction, the sessions often degenerate into dialogues of discouragement that merely rehearse the problem because no one has been recognized or authorized to take the discussion forward to explore solutions. This crucial role of shaping the conversation and providing process consulting seems best played by a neutral party who is skilled enough in collaborative practices to coach the group into action.

When I have participated in collaborative efforts such as these, I've played the role of conversation coach once the other preconditions have been satisfied. Because I didn't have "a fork in the meat"—no organization to promote and no need for local recognition—I was able to move the group from pain to plan. I could put the appropriate considerations on the table without raising suspicions or appearing to hijack the discussion for my own benefit. In my opinion, the usefulness of a neutral coach can hardly be overestimated.

One of the city groups I'm working with got stuck in coming up with a plan. After months of meetings that went nowhere except to rehearse the problem, the local champions called me in for a strategy session. My neutral but active participation changed the dynamics of the session because the group now had to respond to my prodding and my questions. We held a shaped conversation over two hours that coached the participants to identify key elements of an initiative that everyone favored. (These were elements that had been tossed around earlier but never nailed down.) From there, we formed a work group to incorporate the elements into a plan and bring it back to the group for discussion. These simple steps had eluded the group because no one had been positioned to guide the group's attention and conversation. With just a little bit of coaching, the players willingly moved off high center because everyone in the room was committed to going forward.

A fifth precondition I would add is a *convener*. Actually, this element comes first. Someone has to be able to get people into the room. This might be the same person as the champion, but not necessarily. Sometimes the person who can get people to respond to a meeting invitation is not the person to champion the project. Perhaps it is not their passion, or maybe they have too many other responsibilities that prohibit their ongoing engagement. For example, the mayor of my hometown was able and willing to convene two dozen community leaders for a Columbia CityServe project in 2013. No one else could have assembled that team. But his other duties kept him from having much additional engagement with the project. Local champions had to step in at that point to provide the energy and leadership to move forward.

These five preconditions—a convener, local champions, adequate financial resources, a sense of urgency, and a conversation coach—provide the essential elements for an environment in which collective impact has a chance to succeed. But these elements are not all that is necessary for effective cross-domain collaboration to work.

Conditions for Collective Impact

The researchers at Stanford also identified five essential ingredients for collective impact: *a common agenda*, *shared measurements*, *mutually reinforcing activities*, *continuous communication*, and *backbone support*.[3] Again, I find the identification of these crucial conditions to be extremely helpful in my work with community groups. Not only do they give us a language for understanding what must be part of an effective initiative, but they also provide a developmental path that community collaborators can work through to move from pain to plan.

Having a *common agenda* means sharing a vision for change, supported by a common understanding of the problem and substantial agreement on a joint-action approach. Achieving a common agenda often proves difficult, even if a group convenes around a shared concern. For instance, a group's decision to tackle child literacy does not automatically create a common agenda. Multiple issues contribute to a child's capacity to learn. These include parental engagement, the child's readiness (word exposure and preschool development), food challenges, summer reading, and classroom environment. Choosing not to tackle all these factors at once, the groups I've worked with have struggled to come up with specific targets. The key is to gain traction and credibility with a focused initiative. In other words, pick something and do it well. Then the group can expand its efforts.

If you visit the website for Read2Win (www.Read2Win .org), you will discover a focused common agenda championed by a faith-group network in Fort Worth, Texas: to "eradicate illiteracy among elementary schoolchildren" in the Fort Worth Independent School District (FWISD).

This group targets first-grade reading, with the goal of having every first-grade student in the FWISD reading at a first-grade level or above. This focus is not arbitrary. Educators generally agree that a third-grade reading level constitutes the great divide between learning to read and reading to learn. When the Fort Worth crew became aware of this information, they decided to move upstream from the problem and focus on first graders. They work with at-risk students by reading with them each week and working through flash cards to build vocabulary. Developing this shared agenda took months.

Once the organization determined their focus, they met with school officials to hammer out a well-informed approach—their common agenda. To date, they have recruited hundreds of volunteers to read one hour per week (thirty minutes each with two at-risk first graders). Working with the school district, they created a set of flash cards with words that first-graders need to know in order to have adequate word recognition and vocabulary. As of this writing, the Read2Win initiative has readers in about three dozen of the district's eighty-five elementary schools. Some students have come off the at-risk list in as few as six weeks.

Deciding on *shared measurements* enables a community collaborative effort to collect data on a common set of measures to track performance, maintain accountability, accelerate learning, and celebrate progress. Influence Pensacola's summer reading initiative involves collecting more than 100,000 books—three for every child in the elementary- and middle-school population—to be distributed to kids for summer reading. This goal provides a shared measure for success.

The correct shared measurements can reflect established correlations between certain activities and concrete outcomes. For instance, Titus County Cares started by tracking the number of backpacks and the amount of food distributed; now they track test scores, attendance, and trips to the school nurse.

The process of identifying shared measurements can actually help players understand key leverage points that have the greatest impact in crafting solutions for their target problem. Pittsburgh's Promise—a nonprofit foundation that promises students in Pittsburgh, Pennsylvania, a full ride for a college education to any state school in Pennsylvania—provides a great example of this dynamic.

The organization's promise is shared with kids as soon

as they enter school, and it is reiterated throughout each school year. Students are told that the scholarship is theirs, provided that they meet three criteria. First, they must graduate. Second, they must maintain a 3.0 GPA. Finally, they must have at least 90 percent attendance. Because research has shown a direct link between truancy and the failure to graduate, these requirements reflect leading factors in producing eligible recipients. The shared measurements support the strategy. And they produce results! To date, more than four thousand young people have been able to attend college who otherwise would probably not have had a chance.

Effective collective-impact projects use *mutually reinforcing activities* as coordinated efforts to further the plan's goals. For instance, Titus County Reads—a TCC summer reading initiative for school-age children—gathers books from the faith community to distribute to students as they leave for the summer months. But they are also adding an hour of reading to the city-sponsored day camp that runs all summer long during the week. They also seek volunteers to add a reading component to the summer food program that targets kids who receive free or subsidized lunches during the school year. These reinforcing activities will serve to increase the impact of the summer reading initiative.

Mutually reinforcing activities also allow different domains to make distinct contributions to the larger goal. One congregation in Houston, for example, developed a plan for providing an after-school program for underprivileged kids. Their goal was to provide a facility, called a Cy-Hope Center, near each of the forty-plus Title I elementary schools in their district. Church leaders knew they had to have help from other domains in order to put their plan into action. They raised more than one million dollars from business and private donations and also started a community sports league (called Dierker's Champs and headed by former Houston Astros pitcher Larry Dierker). In the after-school program, church members provide tutoring, the regional food bank supplies the food program, and members of the Houston Symphonic Band and a local arts council pitch in with music instruction and art classes. Each Cy-Hope Center represents genuine cross-domain collaboration.[4]

The multiple players in collective-impact projects need *continuous communication* to keep the initiative front and center, provide motivation for continued involvement, and celebrate progress. Obviously, when we think of communication today, we think of informative and interactive websites. But we should also develop social-media strategies to inform and engage people in our cross-domain efforts.

The communication process typically begins even before the common agenda is formalized or the initiative officially gets underway. In the North Oak Cliff community of Dallas, a group representing government, faith, education, and business has been holding conversations for months to determine the feasibility of creating a "day laborer" center. The center would not only serve as a great point of contact for companies that need workers and people who need jobs; it could also serve as a center where educational services such as GED and ESL classes, parenting seminars, and financial instruction could be offered.

These conversations would lack authenticity if they did not include the day laborer population itself, asking them what they would find most helpful and useful. Because one of the goals of this initiative is to aid in building a tighter and more integrative community in the face of shifting demographics and gentrification, the dialogue itself supports the overall effort. Whatever comes out of the discussions will have a stronger chance of success because of the early inclusion of all interested parties.

Finally, cross-domain community development collaboratives require *backbone support* to provide the organization and staff necessary for resource development, project management, communication, and whatever else the initiative needs to be successful. Whereas a stand-alone project can be launched with a single group committed to its success, the sustainability of a collective-impact project depends on finding a suitable backbone organization.

Last spring, a group I worked with in my hometown of Columbia, South Carolina, pulled together a weeklong service effort called Columbia CityServe. Thousands of volunteers gave tens of thousands of hours to clean up neighborhoods and parks, repair homes, donate food, give blood—you name it. We succeeded in getting the mayor and other members of city government involved, along with the University of South Carolina, some local businesses, a few neighborhood associations, and major social-service entities such as United Way and Harvest Hope (our regional food bank).

It was a good effort, but no organization has yet emerged as a viable backbone to sustain the idea. A project of this scope demands a marketing strategy, an online presence, coordination with city and county agencies, volunteer recruitment and training, resource development—in other words, way too much work for a small group of volunteers to accomplish in our spare time, no matter how much enthusiasm we have for the project. We need someone who will wake up every day with the project in mind and the resources at hand.

Three options present themselves when it comes to identifying backbone support in a community. A group can create an organization, which is what the Houston congregation did in creating the Cy-Hope Foundation to support its after-school program. Another strategy is to repurpose an existing organization. This is how Titus County Cares was formed on the back of the local ministerial alliance. A third option is to accelerate or enhance the work of an existing organization. Influence Pensacola was started several years ago as a not-for-profit community development organization. With education and health-care initiatives now coming out of the new cross-domain collaborative effort, the organization has gained traction. Now, Influence Pensacola provides a backbone for multiple community development efforts.

These insights into preconditions and conditions of effective collective impact can help you craft a successful community development initiative in your own town. More than that, they can help you give expression to the Kingdom agenda you want to pursue and help you build a coalition of like-minded Kingdom agents. In short, if you're wondering whether or not you can shift the church narrative into a Kingdom narrative, be encouraged! Not only is it possible, it is being done! You don't have to just read about it; you can jump-start the process in your own community or neighborhood.

Twists and Turns on the Path to Collaboration

As you work to recast the church's narrative as a Kingdom saga, you may encounter a few twists and turns along the way.

1. Expect some pushback from religious people. Don't be surprised if you encounter resistance within the church when you begin seriously re-narrating the church-centered story. Some opposition is inevitable. It may come from people in the community, but more likely it will arise from inside the church. Some of the criticism and objections will be born out of genuine bewilderment and confusion. Remember, the church story has centuries of history and all manner of practical and theological systems behind it. Other resistance may come simply because people prefer the status quo. It's comfortable and familiar, and they know how to operate in the current environment. For many, the institution, with all its trappings, trumps a move toward a people-development agenda.

If you encounter resistance, remember that you are in good company. The religious leaders didn't crucify Jesus for founding the church. They killed him for mounting an assault against their authority and agenda. So count on being tested—maybe a little, maybe a lot. But don't treat every objection or naysayer the same way. It is helpful to know whether you are dealing with late adopters (which is more a function of personality and psychology) or with people who are outright opposed to what you are doing. You can afford to be patient with the first group, but respond to the entrenched opposition swiftly!

2. Beware of non-collaborators. In any group endeavor, there will be those who don't come to the table to collaborate—whether for lack of character, a shortage of collaborative experience, or some other conscious or unconscious motive. If it's only that they have not yet learned how to collaborate, there's hope. After all, most church leaders have been taught to inspire, persuade, and manage a flock within pretty tight parameters. We haven't necessarily been trained in collaborative skills, which may require new competencies. But these abilities can be acquired. Leaders who lack character or who have other priorities in play are a different story. They will impede collaboration by forming coalitions, hijacking ideas, or acting as downright saboteurs. Mark these people as "doesn't play well with others" and be careful not to give them leadership roles and platforms.

I'm working in a city right now where a group is maneuvering to become the backbone support organization for the next phase of a community initiative. They are abusing their planning assignment to craft a strategy suggestion that positions them as the ones in place to take over the initiative. They can be, and must be, reined in at this point so that the common agenda does not fall victim to non-collaborative leaders.

3. Don't reinvent the wheel. This advice seems obvious, but it is too often ignored. For instance, organizations often launch literacy initiatives on top of two dozen reading programs that are already in place. The smart move might be to come alongside or undergird the work of people who are already working at a project. When we don't take this approach, we not only ignore valuable knowledge and insight that can inform our efforts; we also may actually make enemies of people who are on our side!

I remember having coffee with the executive director of a major gospel mission agency in a Southern city. That very day, the mayor had announced a new effort to put together a coalition of leaders to address the city's growing homeless population, as people were flocking to that community.

"We've been in the business of serving the homeless for over seventy-five years," the agency leader told me, "and I wasn't even invited to the meeting." This leader could have contributed significantly to the knowledge pool and experience base. Now, after five years, this community is no closer to solving their homeless problem because there is no intentional, collaborative conversation underway to move the discussion forward.

Asset-based community development is a well-known development strategy based on the idea that the assets needed for tackling and solving issues already exist within the community. Taking the time to compile a full inventory of current initiatives, actions, and available services in your community is a good way to avoid reinventing the wheel. One group decided to create a directory of locally available social services so that community leaders and organizations could refer people for help and cut down on duplication of effort.

4. **Include in the conversation the people you are trying to help.** I really like Larry James's approach at CitySquare in Dallas, where his team fashioned a dynamic, multimillion-dollar cross-domain ministry dynamo from the humble beginnings of a food pantry ministry. One of Larry's themes

is that the poor possess wealth that we ignore when we take the approach of doing things *for* people rather than *with* them. Just because people lack money does not mean they don't have other resources—time, labor, talent, connections, and insights.

People need to participate in their own recovery. Not only does this promote responsibility and accountability, but it also preserves dignity. I worked with an urban church in a decaying section of a Midwestern city. The pastor is a woman with a Kingdom song in her heart. Though only a few dozen people worship there on Sunday mornings, more than three hundred minister there during the week, working to build a better community. Homeless people serve homeless people. That pastor knows that the Kingdom is about developing people, not just doing things for them.

5. Don't be afraid to pull the trigger. I know that responsible leaders want to do their due diligence when considering plans for the future, but an overly cautious approach can inhibit the launching of epic Kingdom adventures. Jesus told us to count the cost of a venture and to size up the opposing forces (Luke 14:28-32), so be smart and don't rush off without adequate information and good scouting reports. But there comes a time when a leader or group of leaders has to say, "Yes!" or "Go!" or "Let's do this!"

Too often, our conversations and best intentions get delayed by "complicators"—people who continually come up with reasons for not moving forward or who take the simple and make it complex. The end result is that the group bogs down or feels exhausted and paralyzed.

Just this week, I have been working with a team on a

project that isn't very complicated. Yet two members of the group pulled me off to the side to voice their concerns about "image" and "budget" and the need for further research. I am no longer surprised when this happens. Lots of people like to jawbone about problems; a lot fewer have the courage to take action.

6. Figure out a good toehold and start climbing. I get this question a lot: "If we want to engage the community with a Kingdom agenda, where's the best place to start?" After decades (even centuries) of focusing on getting the community to connect with the church, church leaders often simply don't know how to connect with the community. My answer is always the same. In terms of helping the church change its storyline to a Kingdom narrative, the local public schools are the best place to start.

Two facts shape my perspective. First, every societal ill in every community manifests itself in the public schools. Broken and dysfunctional families, poor health, destructive lifestyles, institutional and generational poverty, racism, crime—you name it, the consequences show up at school. Second, no other endeavor covers as much of the human landscape as education. Every life and health indicator is tied to education: jobs, well-being, family, even church attendance. When we work to improve education, we touch a lot of other real estate in terms of bettering people's lives.

Schools today face increasing challenges and greater pressure not only to teach but also to parent, mentor, and feed—a seemingly impossible task to do well on all fronts. Schools are a war zone, and we had better get into the fight. The battle for the future of American culture is fought every day in the classrooms and halls, locker rooms and gyms, science labs and cafeterias of our local schools. That's why I urge every congregation to adopt a school. If you can't adopt an entire school, adopt a grade. If you can't adopt a grade, adopt a classroom. If you can't adopt a classroom, adopt a kid or sponsor a teacher. We can all take on this last one, as individuals, without anyone else's help. But can we not also find others to partner with us in this vital endeavor?

Too many church leaders are still under the impression that it's hard for the church to get into the local schools. This dynamic is undergoing rapid change. In just a few short years, we have seen the schools' openness to church involvement skyrocket because of the challenges they face and the help they need. David Staal, president of Kids Hope USA, recently shared with me a statistic that was both encouraging and frightening. His organization helps to pair congregations with schools, training church people to become mentors for students. For years, David's biggest challenge has been to sell schools on the idea of letting churches help. Now, he says, he has more than 1,500 schools on a list awaiting churches as partners. The encouragement is that the school door is wide open. The troubling news is that churches aren't standing in line to serve.

7. **Assume a servant posture.** As Jesus taught us, the way up is down. "How can we help?" is the right question to open up all kinds of Kingdom opportunities. We don't have to figure everything out and then try to get people to want it. Start by asking them what they need! People will tell you. And even if you know you have a lot more to offer, start with what they ask for.

A young Episcopal priest in Dallas told me about visiting the principal at the closest school to his parish house when he was assigned to a new ministry post. He told her he was there to serve the community, not just the church, and he wanted to know how he could help. (What a great example of a Kingdom-centered mentality!) The principal responded by saying she needed a school crossing guard for the early morning drop-off period.

This priest, with hundreds of volunteers potentially at his disposal, possessing all kinds of abilities and resources, could have been offended by this tiny request. Instead, he chose the better response: "Sure!"

The next day, he began his duties . . . and you know the end of this story, don't you? In less than a year, he has become the go-to spiritual advisor anytime anyone has an issue on that campus. He now has deployed dozens of other volunteers into the school. All because he was a servant.

Then there was the church leader who approached a school district in Northern California to see how his congregation could help.

"You Christians stay out of our schools!" a district administrator told him. "I know what you're up to."

That was eight years ago. Today, the church runs the PE program for the entire district, employing dozens of people full-time to spend their days with thousands of students on multiple school campuses. Salt and light was brought in at the district's invitation. This is an amazing story, not just because of the scale of the turnaround but because of how it happened. The church found behind-the-scenes ways to serve the school district, even when initially they were cussed at and thrown out on their ear. They literally served their way into favor.

8. Expect collaboration to be messy. A friend I'm coaching on some community-development initiatives wrote to me this past week. Frustrated by the difficulty of getting groups on the same page in his community, he lamented, "Collaboration is messy." He was right. Competing agendas, lots of distractions, control issues, short attention spans, differing value systems—these are just the tip of the iceberg compared to the challenges you'll face in collaborating with other people. Don't be surprised by that.

If cross-domain collaboration were easy, everyone would be doing it! That's why it's so much simpler to hunker down in our own little bunkers without a thought for how we might tackle much bigger issues.

I do some consulting work for the Salvation Army's eastern-Australia headquarters in Sydney. The Salvos (as they are called there) have garnered an enormous amount of goodwill and respect from their fellow Aussies as a result of their helpful service to the community. As the Army has grown in size and complexity, the leaders have discovered that they can be even more effective by becoming more collaborative in their own delivery systems. For the past two years, they have been redesigning their internal processes around a collaborative "hub" concept that breaks down the walls between the worshiping corps units, the Salvo Stores, the various charity outreaches, and the employment centers they run. This process has proven messy and even contentious at times, but happily they are making progress. The leaders created a campaign for this initiative ("The need is great; we are better together") to communicate both the *why* and the *how* of the hub concept. It takes this kind of focused and determined leadership to work through all the messiness involved in collaboration, to push for better solutions *together* than we can pull off on our own.

9. Don't give up! It takes longer to change than some of us can tolerate, so we're tempted to give up. Don't do it! It can take up to a year to frame a common agenda that can launch a community initiative with a good chance for success. It can take months before we have evidence that what we're doing is making a difference. It can take multiple years to change a church-centered culture. It takes time to rewrite the narrative from a church-centered story into an epic Kingdom saga. Be prepared to spend a lot of time waiting for the world to change while you continue to work every day to make it happen. In the power of the Holy Spirit, your efforts will outlast the opposing forces.

The development of Kingdom collaborations points to a hopeful sign for the church's ability to change its narrative. The "progression of the prepositions," as I call it, holds clues for reshaping the church's story. The church has moved from merely being *in* the community (placing demands on community services while occupying tax-exempt property), to being *for* the community (serving the community through various ministries), to being *with* the community in Kingdom efforts. We come alongside people and organizations to work together *with* them to build a better neighborhood, town, or city. This progression of prepositions has marked a clear path enabling the church to emerge from its citadel, reorient itself to street-level realities, and join the Kingdom party that is already underway.

A collaborative approach bears testimony to the truth that God is *in*, *for*, and *with* us. It acknowledges that he is at work growing his Kingdom. God is calling his people out to play where he is at work. Many are responding. Some are even willing to lead the movement. If you are one of these, the next chapter is for you!

7

MAKING THE MOVE

I WAS INTO THE QUESTION-AND-ANSWER portion of my presentation. All morning, several hundred church leaders had listened to my impassioned appeal to move their congregations into greater missional engagement with their communities. A hand went up at the back of the room.

"What are the obstacles to going missional?"

The question was followed by dead silence; everyone in the room wanted to know the answer.

I paused a moment and then replied: "Every obstacle to your going missional is sitting right here in this room. No one can keep you from going missional. Only *you* can."

It's true. How you live your life and what you choose as your leadership focus are decisions that only you can make.

You will decide whether you will spend your leadership capital on moving those in your constellation of influence into a Kingdom-centered narrative.

This chapter is for everyone who is determined to lead the body of Christ from its current church-centered position into its rightful place and function in the Kingdom saga. Perhaps you serve in a professional staff role or occupy a volunteer leadership role in a ministry organization. Maybe you have no current, formal leadership assignment but still command a following of people who respect your views and will follow your lead.

Having made the decision to pursue a Kingdom agenda, you may ask what will be required of you. Specific skills and strategies will help you in this journey. Your challenge may be all the more daunting because you may have been trained to lead by managing an institution. Now we need for you to lead a *movement*, which requires a very different set of skills and emphases. You will continue to draw on your institutional management experience, and you may still need to manage budgets, supervise staff, crank out sermons, and run programs. But you will also need the aptitude and ability to inspire and lead people (some of whom will be resistant naysayers) through a cultural transformation. That's a tall order, without question.

Moving from a church-centered approach to a Kingdom-centered narrative will demand a complete change of principles, priorities, and practices—in other words, a culture shift. To transform a culture, you must be willing to change your vocabulary, reconfigure your scorecard, and alter your leadership behavior. All three of these changes require deliberate attention. In this chapter, we'll unpack some key insights and offer suggestions in each of these areas. Because many readers will be church leaders, the comments are tailored for application in a congregational setting.

Do You Speak "Kingdom"?

Language not only reflects culture; it creates it. When Starbucks burst onto the scene in the late 1980s, it created a new vocabulary for coffee drinkers. Not that many years ago, no one would have understood what I was talking about if I had asked for a tall skinny decaf mocha latte. (In fact, it took me a while to get it right myself!)

By walking just a few blocks in Manhattan, you can go from Chinatown to Little Italy. Both communities are embedded side-by-side in the same city, but the two areas are cultures apart, with different languages spoken on the streets and displayed on restaurant menus and shop signs. You might as well be in two different worlds.

When considering how language can support a shift in the narrative of the North American church, we must think about both *what* we talk about and *how* we talk about it. Church leaders and congregations who speak *Kingdom* will reflect a profoundly different culture than leaders and congregations who speak *Church*, even though both may be embedded in the same denomination or inhabit the same block in a community.

Much of this book is an attempt to help you with the vocabulary necessary to craft a Kingdom narrative. Here is a summary of the most important "flash cards" you might use to shape your conversation.

The Kingdom of God = life as God intends it. This understanding is foundational to *what* and *how* we think about the Kingdom. Casting the Kingdom in terms of *life* reflects a personal, incarnational (embodied), and organic concept of what the Kingdom is. As one pastor told me, "This perspective allows me to approach and talk about the Kingdom as part of everyday life." Then he added, "People can relate to it!"

The Kingdom saga = the extent to which God will go to make sure we have access to the life he intends for us to experience. This characterization of God's Kingdom activity includes his direct engagement in human history, culminating in the incarnation of Jesus—that is, his life, death, and resurrection. It also includes the efforts of God's people throughout history, as well as the pervasive and residual goodness in the world.

The church = the people of God partnering with God in his redemptive mission in the world. This biblical view of church shifts our understanding of it from *place* and *program* to *a way of being* in relationship with God and humanity. It positions followers of Jesus as coconspirators with God in healing the damage caused by sin. Terms such as "people," "partnering," and "in mission" make it clear that the crosshairs of God's purpose are centered on the *world*, not the church.

Church-centered narrative = the internally focused, programmatic expression of the church. This narrative frames the church as a clergy-dominated organization pursuing ministry that predominantly conducts and celebrates activities aimed at church people, led by church people, and conducted on church property.

Kingdom-centered narrative = the story of God's redemptive work in the world. This redemptive work is present in every domain of human activity, including the intentional engagement of God's people with this mission.

People of blessing = the covenantal role of God's people (Genesis 12:1-2). This phrase characterizes our intended bearing toward the world.

Kingdom of priests = the role extended to every believer in the church. This is a biblical doctrine that supports the work of God's people on behalf of all people in every area of life.

"Life is a mission trip" = a metaphor for why and how we live our lives. This metaphor expresses the intentionality that undergirds a Kingdom perspective.

Language Tips

Here are some things to remember in mastering a Kingdom-centered vocabulary.

- Use *"the* church," not *"a* church," *"our* church," or *"their* church." There is no such thing as *"a* church" in biblical understanding because the use of the indefinite article implies that there are multiple other options. There is only one church, *the* church—the one established by Jesus.

- Use the word *congregation* when referring to a specific gathering of the church. You can pair the words *a, our, my,* or *their* with *congregation* to appropriately designate a distinct gathering of God's people in a specific locale.

- Tell stories of the Kingdom by celebrating ways in which God has revealed himself and his power in and through people's lives.

- In your gatherings, celebrate Kingdom priests who exercise their gifts and callings in deployed-Kingdom settings—that is, out in the world.

- In your gatherings, routinely interview community leaders (the mayor, city council members, school superintendents, police chiefs, local school guidance counselors, principals, etc.) as a way of reminding God's people that the Kingdom saga is actively unfolding in the streets of your town.

You might want to conduct a thorough communications audit of your website, print publications, teaching archives, and videos to make sure they speak Kingdom.

What's the Score?

A second major shift that leaders must address in order to transform the culture of the church involves changing the scorecard. This includes the leaders' personal scorecards as well as the congregation's or ministry organization's corporate scorecard.

Some people object to my use of the term *scorecard*. They believe it connotes competition. If you have a descriptive word you like better, by all means use it; but I'm basically referring to the things we *celebrate*, *reward*, or *value*. It's a fact of human behavior—in the family, at school, and in business—that whatever gets rewarded gets done. Whatever we celebrate—personally or in our organizations—tends to garner attention and resources. And whether we use the word *scorecard* or *celebration* or something else, the truth is that we all have a personal and organizational sense of when we are winning.

In my book *Missional Renaissance* (Jossey-Bass, 2009), I make the suggestion that we need to reallocate resources (the same ones we use to "do church") for greater missional engagement with our communities. These resources are prayer, time, money, people, facilities, and technology. The target of these resources will differ depending on the initiatives, but these are the elements all leaders must work with when they determine their strategies. Consider, for instance, how you would reallocate prayer to support a Kingdom-centered narrative. How would your prayers in your larger gatherings, your small groups, your staff and committee meetings, be different in content? Would you focus on asking for God's help to get "church stuff" accomplished, or would you shift to an external focus? How would your teaching on prayer be altered? You'll want to work through these same types of questions for each of your resource categories.

Please understand, I'm not suggesting that your congregation or ministry organization should stop taking assessments on all internal metrics. My hunch is that you will continue to count the number of people who participate in your programs and activities right along with how much money you are raising. What I *am* suggesting is that the Kingdom results you are after will require a foundational shift in your scorecard.

For instance, increasing numbers of spiritual leaders are shifting their sense of accomplishment away from how many people are in the pews on Sunday mornings to how many are actively deployed in the community during the week and whether the people in the community are living better lives as a result. These metrics include items such as the number of hungry kids receiving food; the number of jobs being created; the reduction in the crime rate; the number of books being collected for summer reading; the number of volunteer service hours being invested in the community; graduation rates; the amount of land under cultivation in urban gardens; the rate of marriage success; the number of kids being adopted out of the foster care system; the number of spiritual conversations taking place throughout the week; and yes, the number of people deciding to become Jesus-followers. The list can—and will—go on, depending on each community's challenges and what breaks the hearts of the local assemblies of Jesus-followers.

As we engage more often in collaborative efforts, we'll begin to experience more "epic wins" related to elements of community development—which means *improving the quality of people's lives* and *bringing the Kingdom to light in our communities*. Those whose focus stays only on the church will find themselves left out of the party. But if we prepare ourselves and our congregations for this development, we will get in on the thrill of seeing the Kingdom of God shrink the territory under domination by the kingdom of darkness.

If you are determined to change the scorecard in your congregation or organization, please understand that you are up against centuries of conditioning that have trained church people to think otherwise. They—*we*—have been taught to view church-centered metrics as the measure for "how our church is doing."

A lay leader lamented to me recently about the decrease in attendance and giving in his congregation. For him, this signaled a losing season. (By the way, he was also blaming the the pastor for this situation.) There was no mystery about this leader's scorecard. So as you seek to bring about a change in mind-set, you will have to be very deliberate—not only in collecting data to support your community engagement and impact but also in finding intriguing ways to report progress, celebrate life transformations, and honor people's contributions. And you will learn to tell stories that signal your gains—or, more accurately, the gains of the Kingdom.

Begin with an honest assessment of your current ministry scorecard. Analyze your current website, print pieces, worship announcements, staff structure, and leadership time allocations to discern what you are currently celebrating. Review your vocabulary, the words and catchphrases you use to describe the church's mission, approach, and objectives. So often our words betray what we're actually thinking and doing.

A thorough budget analysis also will help. One pastor told me that when he counted all the hours involved in producing the weekend worship experience, both his time and the time that other staff members contributed, he discovered to his dismay that 80 percent of the budget went to support this one effort.

This scorecard and budgetary evaluation may include a survey of your constituents, asking them questions such as "What are one to three things you think we (as leaders) see as the most important to our organization?" and "How do *you* measure success in our congregation?" You can conduct this inquiry in small groups, ministry teams, or with the entire congregation. This kind of evaluation will help you determine both how big the challenge will be to change your scorecard and where you might want to focus your efforts to be most effective in bringing about change.

In my experience as a consultant, I've seen that this one issue—changing the scorecard—is often the most challenging part of the cultural shift, at least initially. It requires enormous intentionality and a fair amount of insight to know how to craft new ministry metrics not only to celebrate Kingdom activity and movement in the right direction, but also to honor results. We already know how to measure church participation, but figuring out how to measure and celebrate Kingdom growth is a new and daunting challenge.

Your personal scorecard may also require serious revision. In a conference recently, a young pastor made a statement and then raised a question. "We pastors are pulled by so many different demands. How do you propose we find time to do the things you are talking about in community development?" Before I could answer, another pastor chimed in and said, "We're going to have to make some tough choices. We can't keep doing everything we're doing at church and add this to our plates." He's absolutely right! It takes courage and conviction to change your personal priorities and your ministry scorecard.

Let's face it, many spiritual leaders will be reluctant to make these tough choices, not only because of the resistance they'll encounter from others but also because of the pushback they'll get from themselves! As spiritual leaders, our sense of accomplishment has long been tied to our portfolio of church activities (preaching, leading worship, teaching, pastoral care, small-group leadership, committee administration, and project management, to name a few). We get affirmation for doing these things. Attaching our scorecard to results that take a long time to achieve and might never show up in a church service will not give us the immediate "atta boy!" feedback we desire.

Here's a truth that may help to fortify you for the task at hand. Changing your ministry scorecard is not only a requirement for shifting your ministry culture toward a Kingdom narrative; it also opens the door to a world of energy and renewal as you become a co-conspirator with God as a Kingdom agent. One pastor in his sixties went from saying, "I don't know if I can make it to retirement" (a statement he made in our first conversation), to lamenting, "I wish I had thirty more years to do this" (a comment he made in our latest conversation). The "this" that has brought him such profound personal renewal is a citywide community development engagement with the school system.

I meet pastors and church leaders every week who are struggling with burnout. Church work is just about to take them under. But I don't know a single spiritual leader pursuing a Kingdom agenda who is ready to throw in the towel. Why? Because they stepped into life when they adopted a Kingdom-centered ministry and scorecard.

Ready to join these revived agents of the Kingdom? I have a few more suggestions to help you on your way.

Leading a Movement

Changing your organization's vocabulary and scorecard can carry you a long way toward effecting the culture change necessary to move from a church-centered ministry orientation to a Kingdom-centered one. But without a corresponding third shift, you may never get underway, much less sustain a successful effort in the face of the many challenges you will face. You will probably have to make some changes yourself before you will convince others that you are serious about making the move to a Kingdom agenda.

Here are ten heads-up tips to ensure that you are prepared to lead a Kingdom movement.

1. **Go first.** Whatever you want to see happen, go do it! Movements are not led from the back row or the balcony. They require leaders who are willing to wade into the action, who have the smell of the crowd on them. Your personal commitment will set the tone for the culture and will legitimize your call to action for others. Don't be shy about what you are doing. Share your risks, your discoveries, and your successes along with your frustrating disappointments and failures.

   Your experience in the midst of the fray will not only educate you about what is needed for the movement; it will also help you appreciate the things that people who follow you into action deal with. If I weren't involved in some local community development and educational initiatives in my own hometown, I would have a limited understanding of what the city teams I coach are up against. My own experience at building local, cross-domain collaboratives has acquainted me with city politics, turf wars, communication challenges, and how hard it is to get people mobilized around goals they care about but feel powerless to achieve. But in my consultations now, I can share some things I have learned through my own experience.

2. **Don't go it alone.** When you charge out to engage the community, be sure to grab someone else to go with you. There are a couple of reasons for this. First, no system of disciple-making or mentoring has ever been able to improve upon the apprenticeship model. I recommend to congregational leaders that they routinely scan their organizations for people who are susceptible to the Kingdom virus. Take these people into the battle alongside you. Once they've caught the bug and are contagious themselves, expose them to others who can also catch the fever.

In a congregational setting, this process may follow a scenario similar to one I observed with a client in a Southern city. A schoolteacher struggling to help her congregation become more missionally engaged with the community finally found a seventy-four-year-old team leader who expressed interest in serving as a mentor to at-risk middle school kids. The teacher hooked him up with a mentoring program that trained him and paired him with an eighth-grader who was failing. Not only did this senior member help turn the kid's school life around, he himself experienced a profound spiritual transformation as a result of his involvement.

Imagine the viral power of this man's experience!

First of all, he served as a legitimizer for the new
ministry approach—especially among members of
his generation, who now had one of their own leading the charge. In addition, he embodied the spiritual truth that when we give ourselves away, we find
ourselves. The outgrowth of this powerful story in
that congregation has greatly accelerated the development of a Kingdom narrative in their midst.

3. **Make heroes of the right people.** In a typical
   congregation, the gifts, talents, and energy most
   usually celebrated are those used for conducting
   a worship service or an event that is part of the
   church-centered programming. Thus, we elevate
   the teachers, honor the musicians, thank the
   volunteer labor force, and laud the food-service
   crew that feeds us (usually reserving our longest
   applause for them).

   Though these are not bad things to do, the
   problem is that many congregations never celebrate
   the people engaged in Kingdom ministry in other
   community domains.

   When was the last time you honored a business
   leader for creating jobs or applauded health-care
   workers for their contributions to people's lives?
   Have you ever invited the mayor or a city council
   member to ask about the greatest issues facing your
   community? Or hosted a group of school teachers at
   an appreciation banquet where you pledge to help
   in funding classroom supplies? Many of my clients

make sure that on a monthly basis (at least) they highlight the work of Kingdom priests in the world. Hopefully, this ongoing recognition of the real playing field encourages more people to live out their identity and role as the people of God.

At a meeting of church leaders in Oak Cliff—a community in south Dallas—I met Roberto, a man employed by Southern Methodist University in a community outreach role. Specifically, Roberto helps to organize day-laborer services. He identifies locations where day laborers congregate and helps them to better present their services. He also attends to the other needs peculiar to this population of workers (such as how to avoid getting stiffed for their work). In our conversation, he related to me how important it is for church people to venture into the community to serve. It provides "a new way to see the face of God," as Roberto put it. We have been taught to look for God in the sanctuary, but he is especially active in the streets of our neighborhoods.

4. **Be prepared for conflict.** Don't be surprised that not everyone will want to accompany you on this journey into a more Kingdom-centered universe. This can be true for a number of reasons: fear, prejudice, complacency, apathy, lack of vision, loss of control, loss of identity, unwillingness to engage human need and suffering—any or all of these factors can play a role in making people resistant to

moving away from a church-centered culture. After all, church people know the language and scorecard that support their current worldview. Their resistance is sometimes expressed in a reluctance to participate in community ministry. It sometimes extends into an active campaign to obstruct or upend the new approaches. In its most agitated expression, resistance can be directed at the person(s) responsible for creating the disequilibrium that naturally comes with change, leading to a push for a change of leadership.

I flew out to meet with the leaders and staff of a large congregation that was experiencing turmoil. The senior pastor picked me up at the airport and briefed me on the developments of the previous few months. He had succeeded a long-tenured and highly revered pastor, who had led the congregation for almost four decades. Even though the two pastors had shared senior duties for a year, it was obvious that the transition was not going as planned. The retiring pastor clearly did not relish losing his ministry platform, and the successor was determined to chart a different course during his tenure. The inevitable result was conflict.

The problem was that no one had prepared the leaders, staff, and congregation for these difficulties. After decades of following a skillful leader, everyone was unaccustomed to this level of tension. They automatically blamed the new guy because he was the one introducing all the change. In the ensuing months, the conflict came to a head. Predictably, with no one to appropriately manage their expectations and walk them through the unavoidable shifts and shimmies of a leadership change, they "got rid of the problem"—the new pastor. Another "unintentional interim" bit the dust. This unfortunate but all-too-common outcome could have been avoided if the leaders had not been caught flat-footed by conflict.

5. **Educate yourself about change and transition leadership.** Navigating conflict is part of a much larger set of specific competencies required of leaders who want to navigate from a church-centered to a Kingdom-centered ministry. You will also have to become skilled at managing change and transition—especially if you want to take others along with you.

Change and transition are not the same thing. Change is what happens to us—an external event, force, or decision over which we may have limited or no control. Our favorite restaurant closes. Our best friend dies. A new industry employing thousands of workers relocates to our town. Our internist notices something that doesn't look right in our blood work. Version 12.0 of some technology debuts. These things happen and our world changes, a little or a lot. Everybody knows that change is inevitable.

Transition, on the other hand, is how we process change. It is the internal and psychological mechanism by which we come to grips with a new reality and cope with its implications. It involves emotion.

As leadership consultants often point out, it's not the change that topples a leader; it's the transition. Helping people deal effectively with change can make or break even the best idea—and the leaders behind it.

Leading change and transition is not alchemy. Effective leaders employ identifiable skills and informed strategies to help them survive and even thrive during periods of great change. It takes a blend of emotional intelligence, empathy, toughness, and tenacity to lead people through times of significant transition. Knowing how to "sell the problem" so that people can own it (and therefore own the proposed solutions, as well); understanding and dealing with the causes of resistance; knowing how to deal with tension without escalating conflict; being able to create urgency and establish momentum; anticipating when to move people from pain to plan—leaders need all these abilities to transition people through the rapids of significant change.

Fortunately, help is available in this area. I have found that business consultants offer great insights into change management and transition leadership. John Kotter, William Bridges, Cynthia Scott, Dennis Jaffe, Ronald Heifetz, and Robert E. Quinn are just a few of the writers and thinkers with great insight into this topic. Businesses deal with change on an ongoing basis. The same knowledge and competencies that aid business leaders can help spiritual

leaders because people act like people everywhere—
even in the church!

I recommend that you include others in this
educational process. Don't make it a solo journey.
Whether you are leading a small group or an entire
congregation, helping your leadership team prepare
for transition and change can spell the difference
between success and failure as you seek to navigate
the new world. When people understand that conflict and tension are a necessary (or at least natural)
part of the transition process and not a sign that
something's wrong, they're much less likely to jump
to unwarranted conclusions when the emotional
temperature begins to rise.

6. **Sing your song.** If you're going to lead in changing
the narrative of the North American church, you
will have to lead with conviction. In other words,
you must believe in what you're doing before you
can convince others. Find out how the story works
out in your own life and how it finds expression in
your own message. The words and phrases that you
use, a particular hallmark of your leadership style, or
the kind of environment you shape around yourself
will communicate your personal vision to the people
you're leading.

The tune must resonate with your own life story.
In other words, find strategies and methods that fit
with who you are. One leader I work with views
human creativity as a way to demonstrate Kingdom

life. As an author and playwright, he has fashioned a congregational culture in which people are encouraged to write poetry, compose songs, and create videos as integral pieces of their spiritual formation. These are often highlighted in corporate worship gatherings. Artists in the community have gravitated to this leader and culture, and they are frequently given opportunities to display their work in the church's facilities as well as in art shows organized by the congregation.

Another one of my friends, a well-known pastor, sums up his mission as "helping people find their way back to God." This phrase reveals his motivation and clarifies his objectives. It is the song in his heart that has worked its way out and now shapes every aspect of his vision and ministry. Every member of the congregation he leads learns how they can help others on the journey toward God. Every activity and ministry initiative has the desired end in mind.

For me, since my college days I have had a question that haunts me when my mind is free of other preoccupations: "How can the church be the church?" I cannot tell you the origin of this quest, except to say that I know it's from God. I cannot *not* pursue the answer—not when I was a pastor and denominational leader, and not now as a consultant and leadership coach. No matter my role or assignment, I hum this tune. It is my song. I have to sing it. Paradoxically, my musings on church mission have shown me that the only way the church can be the church is to move past the current church-centered self-absorption into a Kingdom orientation. We are the church only in relation to the Kingdom.

Whatever your own song is, it will ground you, sustain you, and draw others to you who can harmonize with you. If you haven't yet learned what your song—your life message—is, try this: Ask some people who know you the best to tell you what they believe you stand for, what your life goal is, and what motivates you. This information will at least help you discover how you come across to the people you lead. Their answers may yield important clues to help you articulate your life message.

One caveat: Don't try to sing someone else's song. Producing a "cover album" of other people's songs and dreams will not be nearly as robust as the tune you are designed to carry.

7. **Pay attention to what breaks your heart.** Sune Andersen serves as executive pastor of a thriving evangelical congregation, composed of a network of missional communities in Denmark. A few years ago, Sune moved his family into a high-rise apartment building in a less affluent part of their town. He immediately set out meeting his new neighbors, one of whom—the one who lived right next to him—loved to host parties that started late in the evening and lasted far into the early hours of the morning. This posed a challenge for Sune's family because they had a school-age child whose sleep was being disrupted.

The Andersens invited this neighbor over for dinner. During the meal, their new acquaintance began telling his story. Abused and abandoned as a young child, this man had practically raised himself in the streets. Not only had he become a drug user, but he had also moved into trafficking drugs with a network of people who enjoyed coming to his parties.

In recounting this dinner conversation to a group of American pastors, Sune said, "As I listened to this man's story, my heart broke for him." He went on to say, "At that moment my neighbor moved from being a problem to being a person." Quickly he added, "You will go missional at the point your heart breaks."

I have never forgotten this profound insight by this Danish pastor. I tell the story often and sometimes ask people to identify what breaks their hearts. On one such occasion, a woman approached me after the session and quietly confessed, "What breaks my heart is that nothing breaks my heart." She went on to say, "I've got some serious heart work to do." Her candid admission can serve as a point of growth.

So—what breaks your heart? What pulls at your heartstrings? What keeps you up at night or gets you up early in the morning? You should pay attention to what your heart tells you. This insight will give you the passion and energy to remain in the Kingdom business. This is the light you want to add, the darkness you want to quell, and the work you do together with God to aid the coming of the Kingdom on earth.

8. **Become employable.** This advice is for those who
   serve in professional ministry roles. My intention is
   not to come across as negative or disheartening. I'm
   not saying that transitioning to a Kingdom-centered
   narrative will cost you your current leadership
   role. I intend this suggestion to serve as a proactive
   preparation for the future. You may be able to draw
   support from a congregation or other ministry to
   support your livelihood. But I'm confident that more
   and more spiritual leaders will not be positioned in
   full-time church jobs to run church programs.

   This development will not be all bad. The new
   reality will set many leaders free, especially those who
   have Kingdom songs to sing but who serve among
   people whose receivers are not tuned to the same
   frequency. Every week, it seems, I hear a similar sentiment from current church leaders: "If I knew something else to do that would feed my family, I would
   do it." This feeling of being trapped in the church-
   centered culture does not promote emotional health.

   So, become employable. Take some online courses,
   pick up a hobby that can be monetized, talk to a
   career assessment counselor, and figure out the skills
   and talents you currently use that can transfer to other
   jobs (project management, volunteer recruitment and
   training, motivational speaking, etc.). Remember, how
   God funds your ministry may not involve a church
   payroll check. Even if it takes several years to reposi-
   tion yourself, gain credentialing, or add to your skill
   set, you will feel more freedom knowing that you are

working a plan to be able to fund your Kingdom calling in more than one way.

I know a leader who served in various church roles for several years after coming out of the business world. Though he was successful in his various assignments, the church culture just didn't fit him. In his late forties and early fifties, he pursued a counseling degree online and took the plunge into a field that brought him much fulfillment. He was already doing a lot of counseling as part of his church roles. He just needed credentialing to enable him to step outside his church role. Today, he is an international leadership coach to companies on three continents. He is fulfilled; and as a Kingdom agent, he is on the front lines, able to have significant spiritual conversations with business executives who never attend church gatherings.

9. **Be patient with yourself and others.** Sometimes I find myself becoming impatient with people who "just don't get it." I have to remind myself that there was a time when I really didn't "get it" either. People are at all different stages of the journey. The Holy Spirit is leading all of us along, some faster than others. I need to extend grace to others. After all, we have been developing the church-centered narrative for 1,700 years! People in our congregations are only doing what someone told them to do to be good church members. It's going to take more than a few months to turn this thing around. In my work with

congregations, I tend to think in terms of three to five years for a turnaround, and I advise constant vigilance all along the way to avoid the "snap back" to old behaviors and thinking. Patient training, retraining, and visiting and revisiting these truths and themes will be required.

10. **Face your fears.** Some years ago, I was closing down my office to start a vacation when an e-mail hit my inbox. "Dear Brother McNeal," it began, before proceeding into a tirade telling me that lots of people were upset at what I was doing in my role as part of a denominational planning process. The e-mail raised a bunch of issues, none of which I had time to deal with at that moment. I fired off a response, telling the sender that I was headed out of the country and would be in touch with him upon my return.

Three days into the trip, still simmering about the e-mail, I told my wife, "I just can't get that e-mail off my mind."

After I reminded her of its contents, she said, "Reggie, what if he's right?" When she saw me flinch and realized how I had taken her remark, she added, "I'm not talking about his *opinion* of what you're doing. I'm asking you what difference it would make if a lot of people actually *are* upset about what you're doing. Would you change your mind? Would you do anything different than what you are doing now?"

"No," I replied.

"Then what's the worst thing that can happen to

us? You lose your job? Do you think the Lord would look after us?"

Wow! I had been stewing over that e-mail for three days, and in less than a minute, Cathy cut straight to the chase: I was afraid! My anger was a fear response.

My wife gave me a great gift that day. She called out the dragon of fear, and once it had been exposed, she said, in essence, "Look—that puppy's got no teeth!"

The enemy whose kingdom we are invading traffics in fear. He whispers fear into our souls whenever he can. Sometimes, he gets very specific; more often, he just likes to create unsettling background noise in our souls to causes anxiety.

"They will never let me do this."

"I can't get another job."

"I don't have what it takes to pull this off."

These fears bounce around the corridors of our hearts when we contemplate leading a Kingdom movement. Name that fear! I promise you—no, better yet, *Jesus* promises you—that those puppies have no teeth. God understands our predicament. This is why "fear not" is the most frequent command in Scripture. Usually, the command is coupled with the best news: "I am with you." God's presence, coupled with the perfect love he has for you and me, drives out fear.

God wants you—yes, *you*—to experience life as he intends it. God's mission on planet Earth extends all the way to you. It is not something "out there" to pursue. It is *in you*.

You are not incidental to your leadership. Ultimately, the

best strategy for leading those around you into the Kingdom saga is for you to "get it" and "live it" yourself. A truly alive leader serves as a floodgate for the Kingdom of Heaven to pour into this world. Can you think of a better way or reason to live?

So get out there and lead the charge! A better life awaits people—including you! —who need to experience what God intends for them.

8

WHAT NOW?

IF YOU FIND YOURSELF agreeing with most of what this book proposes, you might be wondering, *What do I do now?* The challenge might seem a bit overwhelming or intimidating.

To help you take the next step, I want to offer some suggestions tailored to the two main target groups this book addresses: church leaders (clergy, paid staff, and church ministry leaders), and other Jesus-followers who are intrigued by the potential of living as Kingdom agents. Together, these two groups represent the innovators and early adopters necessary to start a Kingdom-centered movement. If you get the ball rolling, others will join in.

These ideas echo our earlier discussions. Be certain to read all the recommendations, because you might find something in the other group's list that you want to incorporate into your own actions. My goal in writing this final chapter is to show that making the movement from a church-centered agenda to a Kingdom-centered one is doable.

Let's get started.

To Current Church Ministry Leaders

One of the early reviewers of this manuscript raised a couple of questions as part of his feedback: "How can the church be at the center of a movement to get the church out of the center of the movement?" and "How can pastors, who are at the center of the church-centered paradigm, lead us out of that paradigm?"

Great questions. No one said this was going to be easy! To realign the North American church with God's Kingdom story will require leaders who have courage born of conviction and clarity of vision. We need for them to live their lives as stirring examples of their aspirations so that the people they call to follow them will know what they are choosing.

The previous chapter identified some fundamental guidelines that leaders must adopt in order to lead a Kingdom movement. Here are some practical considerations as you get underway.

> • *Pray with greater Kingdom consciousness.* If Jesus instructed us to pray "your Kingdom come," he must have thought it was important. Specifically, your prayers might go something like this: "Lord, help me to earnestly look for your Kingdom today. Open my eyes to see what you see. Open my ears to hear

what you hear. Open my heart to care about what you care about. Don't let me miss what you are doing in the world around me." You might want to keep a journal to record God sightings and God promptings. (If you start filling the pages, you may want to make this a regular practice.) Go back periodically and read through what you've written to see if there are any patterns. God may be whispering—or even shouting—to get your attention.

• *Find other people who "get it."* You're going to need collaborators to provide moral support, generate new ideas, and generate collective energy for tackling Kingdom agenda items. You could start a study group and begin to have conversations about the Kingdom agenda items that seem to catch people's attention in your group. You certainly want to engage like-minded and *life*-minded people in your congregation, but don't stop there. If you're a pastor, look for other pastors in your community who might be having similar thoughts. If the pastors in your area tend to be isolated and non-collaborative, you may need to seize the initiative and knock down some silo walls. It may take several breakfasts or lunches to break through the fog of church-business-as-usual to find out what is really cooking on the hearts and minds of your fellow clergy. One good way to convene a group is to call other pastors to come together to pray for the prosperity of the city. You will find out quickly how high a priority this is for other leaders.

• *Start some new conversations*—with community leaders, school administrators, law enforcement officials, business owners, city officials, health-care professionals, and other service providers. Ask them to identify one or two issues in your community that, if addressed, would make the most difference in your city. You might discover an opportunity for an "epic win" that can become a rallying point to forge a wider collaborative initiative. Also, ask them to identify the problem or issue to which they would most like to devote their own energies. You may be able to connect a few of these leaders to others with similar passions and interests. You can always ask, "How can I be praying for you in your leadership role in our community?" One pastor told me that he had begun going into businesses and asking the owners how he could pray for their business to prosper. In a matter of a few years, he had become the informal chaplain to more than a dozen businesses in town.

• *Get outside more.* If you are a full-time pastor or church staff leader, you may need to get beyond the four walls of your church facility more often. Join a health club or community sports team. Volunteer at a school. Enroll in a college class. You will be amazed what you discover when your world becomes less church centered and insular.

This shift will accomplish several things. First, by having conversations with people outside the church you will discover what's on their minds.

This knowledge may cause you to reflect on your current church priorities.

Second, your ministry will be vastly expanded. The house next door to our daughter and son-in-law's home burned down a couple of years ago, putting their own home at considerable risk in the process. The experience was terrifying. The first-responder they had the most contact with turned out to be a local pastor who was the volunteer chaplain for the local fire department. He ministered not only to the firefighters but also to my family during this particularly scary set of circumstances.

Third, you will experience a psychological lift by cultivating other areas of life besides what's happening in your church programs.

• *Pick a small, sure-win project that doesn't require much funding or deliberation.* This might be a community service, a clean-up day, a teacher move-in support day, or an appreciation dinner for emergency responders. The idea is to build momentum for community engagement and to bolster the congregation's confidence in its capacity to be people of blessing. As you build on these positive experiences, you will create a narrative that supports a Kingdom-centered agenda.

• *Rethink and redesign your current church-ministry programs to reflect a Kingdom bias.* You can make lots of small, incremental adjustments that will add up to a shift in the conversation. Invite community leaders to your weekly gatherings on a routine basis.

Interview them about the issues they deal with and pray for them. Give people a chance to respond to these needs. I have been in places where one simple act created enough missional momentum to change the tenor of the congregation.

Don't stop with your weekly gatherings. Figure out how your website can become a portal for community volunteering. Integrate opportunities for serving children and youth in the community into your children's and youth ministries page. Find more and more ways for ministry activities to be open to the community, not just "club members." You might even develop a scorecard that celebrates shutting down some ministries so that resources can be redirected into missional engagement with Kingdom-life initiatives.

• *Make sure that every church ministry you're a part of is growing in its Kingdom bias.* You may not be the pastor, but perhaps you serve on the stewardship committee. What a great place of influence to introduce Kingdom-focused thinking and practice! Maybe you serve as a church council member who oversees all aspects of the church, or you lead a small group of a dozen participants. Whatever the scope of your leadership, see yourself as a viral Kingdom agent with an opportunity to spread Kingdom priorities to other people and programs. Use your position to set the agenda to pray for your city, to be aware of need, and to mobilize and release the church into its appropriate Kingdom business.

• *Don't make this a solo journey.* Be sure to involve your inner circle in the Kingdom conversation, as well as any key legitimizers or other significant players. You will need these people's support in order to spread your ideas throughout the organization. If you encounter significant resistance to this new direction, you will want to have others standing with you in taking a Kingdom position. Most important, you want the people around you to adopt the Kingdom agenda not because it is *your* vision but because they believe that moving in a Kingdom direction is *God's* vision and mission.

• *Look for points of entry for the Kingdom virus.* A leader in a group I mentor lives in a town of several thousand. Over the past few months, more than a dozen people in the community have died from drug overdoses. Each new death raises awareness among a growing percentage of the town population to this problem. This leader called for a community-wide prayer walk. More than one hundred people of all ages showed up—and not just people of faith or people from one congregation. This leader understands that the epidemic of drug-induced deaths must be combated with a dose of the Kingdom. A second prayer walk she has planned will no doubt draw even more townspeople.

God does not work exclusively through formal leaders to get his work done. But a lot of times he does. The Bible and Christian history are replete with evidence of the positive influence that leaders can have in helping guide God's people and in blessing the world. Those of us who are charged with leadership responsibility in any part of the life of the church have the unique challenge of steering the church in a new direction. We don't need just a change in methodology. We need a transformation of our mission. We have to get beyond thinking and behaving as if the church is God's great mission. The *Kingdom* is the story we need to study and tell.

Leaders who grasp this truth can make a difference. I know because I'm around some of you!

To Intrigued, Inspired, and Intrepid Jesus-Followers

What if you're a leader without a formal, institutional-church leadership role? Maybe you no longer even attend congregational gatherings or participate in church activities. Or maybe you're in church every Sunday, but you see the world with Kingdom vision. You believe that God is actively working in people's lives in every area of human activity. You resonate with the Kingdom message of this book. You are ready to become a more viral Kingdom agent than ever. What difference can you make, and how can you get going (or accelerate your efforts)? As a young professional asked me in a personal coaching session, "How can I use my career to affect the Kingdom without being cheesy?"

Here are some suggestions for you in moving forward.

- *Don't wait for the world to change.* Waiting for your congregation, your small group, your family, or anyone else to "get it" before you get going can too easily become an excuse for inaction. You are a responsible steward of your own convictions. Take action.

• *Order your prayer life around the Kingdom.* If Jesus told us to seek first the Kingdom of God, our prayer lives are a good place to start. Ask God to give you Kingdom eyes so that you can see what's going on in the lives of people around you. Be sensitive to the Holy Spirit's prompting to pray prayers of blessing for your family, coworkers, neighbors, and even your chance encounters. One man told me that when he heard me speak about becoming people of blessing, he felt convicted to bless his teenage son, who was actively rebelling in every area of his life. When his son agreed to allow him to pray a blessing over him, the father placed his hands on his son's head and spoke words of affirmation. The episode was a bit awkward, and neither father nor son felt a seismic shift as a result. But two weeks later, when the dad again offered to bless his son, the boy came and knelt down in front of his father to receive it. This ongoing practice has changed the tenor of their conversations. The boy is still rebellious, but the relationship between father and son is weathering the storm.

• *Keep a thirty-day journal of God sightings and Spirit nudges.* At the end of thirty days, evaluate what you have written to see if any patterns have emerged—of encounters, reactions, or increased awareness. These dynamics can be clues to how God is prompting you to pursue a Kingdom agenda in your world of

work, neighborhood, community, home, leisure—
everywhere you live life.

• *Invite others in.* Host your neighbors for an informal
wine-and-cheese, beer-and-pretzels, or tea-and-
crumpets gathering—whatever fits your lifestyle. Or
take the plunge and do what one couple I know did.
They had recently relocated and were doing a good bit
of business with a local furniture store in town. Over
a few weeks, they developed relationships with two of
the store clerks who had worked closely with them.
They decided to invite them over for a barbecue, and
both clerks accepted on the spot!

One of the clerks said she had lived in the town for
more than four years and had never once been invited
to someone's home; the other clerk was going through a
divorce and was eager for social contact. Two days later,
when the couple returned to the store, the manager
approached them and asked if they were the ones who
had invited some of his employees to a barbecue. Unsure
of his motive, the couple answered a bit tentatively that
they had wanted to show their appreciation for the good
service they had received. To their surprise, the manager
asked if he could come over sometime as well! The couple
wound up inviting all of the store's employees for a party.
The manager closed the store an hour early to make sure
there would be plenty of time for everyone to attend.

Not long after that, the woman who was going
through a divorce asked the wife if just the two of
them could have coffee sometime soon.

When I heard this story, it occurred to me that this couple must have been winsome and inviting, or their invitations would have fallen flat. The way we treat other people in the routine interactions of life will either enhance or diminish our capacity to bless them.

• *Ask yourself the question, "What breaks my heart?"* What issues or concerns or societal ills give you "heartburn"—the feeling that *something should be done?* Pay attention to those feelings. They could be giving you hints about an area of Kingdom engagement that God has lined up for you.

• *Take action on your passion or your pain.* Ask God to direct you, and then initiate something. Approach a local school, Habitat for Humanity, Red Cross, or Salvation Army as a volunteer. Create the margin of time you need by rearranging your priorities. Cut down on spending if necessary to generate money for your projects. In other words, make the necessary and appropriate behavior shifts to allow yourself to pursue your desire to help. One young man I know took a year to raise support so he could quit his job and devote his efforts full time to build and operate an after-school mentoring program in an under-resourced part of my hometown. Because he was willing to put his plans into action, he now runs an after-school program helping more than three dozen children to have a safe place to play, a snack, help with their homework, and a mentor to guide them.

• *Determine (as much as possible) what results you want to accomplish with your efforts.* For instance, do you want to help one child come off the at-risk list for reading, or do you want to galvanize a group of volunteers to achieve this for a classroom or even an entire school? Is it important for you to develop a personal relationship with someone you help, or are you more determined to influence an entire organization? Are you best suited to be a one-person wrecking crew, or are you able to raise an army? Knowing these things will allow you to monitor results and celebrate progress, both of which are critical to your ongoing motivation and success.

• *Honestly assess what you bring to the table.* The conversation in the American workplace in recent years has focused increasingly on helping people discover and work from their personal strengths. This emphasis acknowledges that people are likely to make their best contributions in areas where they are already effective, committed, and motivated. The same dynamic can be applied to our Kingdom efforts in serving others. Figure out ways to help and serve others that use your natural strengths, interests, and abilities. When you serve, bring your best ideas and efforts. Our talents have been given to us by God so we can use them to bless others. Moving in your areas of strength will open the floodgates for the Kingdom to pour through you and into the world.

• *Figure out what you need to learn in order to make your best contribution.* Do you need to become educated on illiteracy—both its causes and cures? Do you need to find out what your strengths are? Do you need to unlearn some prejudices and biases that hinder your Kingdom impact? Should you go back to school to pick up some skill or knowledge? I recently met a woman who is leaving a very successful business to pursue a social-entrepreneurial project. As part of her preparation for the new venture, she is going back to school to pick up some management and sociology classes.

• *Build and surround yourself with a community of like-minded people.* You're not going to pull together a Kingdom-centered lifestyle all by yourself. You will need to collaborate with other Jesus-followers—for accountability, synergy, celebrating the journey, praying for one another, and lightening the load. This is *the church* in its New Testament expression. The Kingdom enterprise is a *team* enterprise.

• *Start where you are.* God is not caught off guard by your current location and life assignment. He might even have had a hand in it! It would be just like God to position you where he needs a Kingdom agent and then patiently bring you along. In other words, you don't necessarily have to disrupt your current life and *go* somewhere to establish a Kingdom work. Start in your own neighborhood or community, in your workplace, with your current relationships. And don't forget your family! More and more families are waking up to the truth that serving together is a key aspect of faith development. Though it's possible that your

Kingdom journey may involve an adventure halfway around the world, don't rush away from your home or local community without taking a good look around.

• *Invite non–Jesus followers into your Kingdom journey.* Remember, God is at work in every single person on the planet. People don't have to adhere to a prescribed set of spiritual beliefs or be at a certain point of relationship with God for him to use them as part of his Kingdom efforts. God's way of connecting with people may involve your including them on a community-development project. Organize a service project for your coworkers. Train for and run in a charity marathon together. Don't be afraid to have conversations about what you experience together, as well as *why* you are doing it.

God conversations will naturally come up as you work alongside other people—especially in serving. Your job is to be ready to give an answer for the hope that is in you. So much negativity permeates our culture. People are drawn to others who radiate hope. I can't think of a better way to invite someone into a spiritual conversation than to create an environment where it will inevitably occur. This is an entirely different approach to evangelism than trying to create an artificial conversation in order to dump a load of spiritual truth on someone.

We must be able to tell our stories with light and love. Just this week, I had dinner with a man who told me how God had completely changed the lives of his alcoholic parents when he was a teenager. No matter what anyone else says, this guy has a story he can't not tell. It involves the Kingdom of God radically altering his family and his own life trajectory. That's powerful stuff! Our non-Jesus-following friends and coworkers need to hear stories like this, which is why we need to invite them into our lives.

To Everyone

This book has been about getting the church to tell a different story. It's about the Kingdom saga, a narrative that swoops from heaven to earth and back. It's a story that catches us up in the telling. And it's a story whose ultimate ending we know, even though its various plots and subplots may not be known in our lifetime.

A man named John Moniz, for example, did not live to see the ninth-grade African-American young man he befriended become the first black senator from the state of South Carolina (my home state). Years ago, John owned the Chick-fil-A restaurant in Citadel Square Mall in Charleston. He began to notice that young Tim Scott, who worked as a ticket-taker at the mall's multiplex, came into the store every day but only ordered French fries and water. One day, John asked the young man why he never ordered anything else.

"Because that's all I can afford," Tim responded.

At that moment, John made a decision that changed the course of a lot of lives. He grabbed a couple of chicken sandwiches and followed Tim out into the mall. As the two sat and ate, they began a relationship that evolved into a weekly meeting. That mentoring relationship eventually led to Tim's high school graduation (at the time he met John, he had been in danger of dropping out of school), followed by a college education, followed by a business venture, followed by entering into public service as a local elected official. On top of it all, John showed Tim how to become a Jesus-follower.

When Tim Scott took the oath of office as a United States senator on January 3, 2013, he said, "Besides Jesus Christ, I want to thank two people for helping me get here: my momma and John Moniz." John died almost two decades ago. He never got to see the full impact he'd had on the life of Tim Scott.

What can you do with a couple of chicken sandwiches? You can change the world, that's what!

So what now? It's up to you—and God, of course. The two of you are coauthoring your life story. I recommend that you center the action on co-laboring with God to give people the chance to experience life as he intends it. You don't have to know the full impact of what you do. You just have to say *yes* to the King and trust him for the results.

It will be quite a saga. A compelling Kingdom story!

CONCLUSION

THE E-MAIL ATTACHMENT CONTAINED the schedule for a conference where I would be speaking a few weeks later. The organizers wanted me to be aware of all the topics that would be addressed by the other speakers so I would know the scope and direction of the discussion. My own assignment was to help the conferees understand their communities better.

As I scanned the list of topics, two session titles caught my attention. The first was "The Primacy of the Church," which would lead off the conference. Later in the program would come "The Importance of the Kingdom."

In the order of presentation, I saw an apt illustration of the plight of the North American church. "Primacy" trumps "importance."

The current story is centered on the primacy of the church. It should be centered on the Kingdom. Far too many leaders and congregations view the church as most important. The Kingdom occupies a lesser spot on the dais.

This places the church as an institution in an idolatrous position. Not only are the people of God not living out their true identity and role in the world; in many ways they are running a counterfeit mission in competition with the mission of God. While God seeks, through the deployment of his Kingdom people, to bring abundant life to the people he created, the church is often too occupied with its own organizational needs and development to join him in his efforts. Community engagement and loving one's neighbors are seen as something to consider after we take care of church business.

This orientation is wrong. I wrote this book to challenge this way of thinking and to help church leaders rediscover their true mission—leading God's people to partner with him in his redemptive efforts in the world. In other words, I'm calling the church to join forces with God in seeking first his Kingdom.

Above all else, I have tried to convey two things: *hope* and *urgency*. Hope that Kingdom agents can make a quality-of-life difference in our communities. Hope that church leaders who want to make the shift from Churchianity to a Kingdom-centered agenda will do so. Hope because I know that God's people are willing to follow Kingdom leadership; they just need to be given the opportunity. Hope that individual Jesus-followers will decide to live their lives on the King's mission to bring life to their communities and neighborhoods. Hope that *you* will say yes and will take others along with you on your journey.

But I also must sound a note of urgency. Urgency that the church must rethink its church-centered narrative *soon* if it is to have any chance of rejoining God's agenda and having a positive impact on our culture. Urgency that the millions of people bundled up inside the church have bigger dreams for their spiritual lives than what they can experience by merely helping a professional clergy achieve religious organizational goals. And urgency that our communities are growing increasingly desperate for the abundant life of Jesus to bring about cultural and individual transformation.

I don't think we have long to change our story. For our country's sake—and for the sake of the church—the time is *now*.

In the evangelical church world in which I grew up, urgency and hope were connected with personal salvation and life in the hereafter. We were encouraged to "invite Jesus into our hearts." This, we were told, was what it meant to "receive Christ."

That perspective, however, is a devastating misunderstanding of the spiritual dynamic and life that Jesus offers. That view reduces Jesus to an additive for the lives we're already living, an app that fails to affect the fundamental operating platform of our lives. When we download salvation for personal consumption, it's not connected to the larger mission of God's Kingdom.

The truth is, we have been invited into God's life. Jesus has invited us into his own heart. *He* has received *us*! It's *his* life that he wants us to experience. He's not an app. He's the operating platform. When Jesus said, "I am the way, the truth, and the life," he meant what he said. What Jesus has in mind for you—for both of us—is no less than sharing his life with you, me, and the world. The opportunity to experience life as God intends it is the *hope* for the world. It is *urgent* that you and I adopt the Kingdom approach to how we live.

In the end, all of this discussion boils down to the good news about the life-giving power of the Kingdom. It is *life* that God desires for us. Our hope is that abundant living really is possible; our urgency is to experience that life. These elements propel us forward in our spiritual quest.

Nothing less than the Kingdom of God will satisfy our dreams, make sense of our experiences, and allow us to become *us*. We were created for the Kingdom. That is why we are desperate until we find it. And once we do, we have a responsibility to show the way to others and to help them on their way to finding it. Following that Way will lead us home!

How's that for a story?

NOTES

CHAPTER 1: MY JOURNEY INTO THE KINGDOM

1. For the characterizations of church as *place* and *vendor*, I am indebted to George Hunsberger's chapter "Missional Vocation: Called and Sent to Represent the Reign of God" in *The Missional Church*, ed. Darrell L. Guder (Grand Rapids: Eerdmans, 1998), 77–109.

CHAPTER 3: THE HEROIC KINGDOM NARRATIVE

1. See www.lenscrafters.com/onesight?sid=OurVisionDD-LeftLink-OneSight -US-112413 and onesight.org.
2. See, for example, http://alphasigmaphi.org/Websites/alphasigmaphihq /images/Officer_Resources/Community_Service_and_Philanthropies.pdf, and https://gohardgreek.wordpress.com/2012/02/04/15-community -service-ideas-for-sororities-and-fraternities-that-combat-hunger-and -homelessness.
3. For more information about the Christian Community Development Association, see http://ccda.org.
4. Learn more about combating human trafficking at http://courage worldwide.org.
5. See, for example, Ladd's *The Presence of the Future: The Eschatology of Biblical Realism* (Eerdmans, 1996).
6. Walt Whitman, "O Me! O Life!" *Leaves of Grass* (1892).

CHAPTER 4: CHALLENGING THE CHURCH'S STORYLINE

1. Billy Graham, as related by his daughter Gigi Graham-Wilson, chapel interview at Asbury Theological Seminary, April 10, 2014.
2. See Paul G. Hiebert, "Set Theory and Conversion," http://hiebertglobal center.org/blog/wp-content/uploads/2013/04/Lecture-Note-36-Set-Theory -and-Conversion.pdf; and Paul G. Hiebert, "Conversion, Culture and Cognitive Categories," http://danutm.files.wordpress.com/2010/06 /hiebert-paul-g-conversion-culture-and-cognitive-categories.pdf.

CHAPTER 6: WHEN IT WORKS: KINGDOM COLLABORATION

1. For more information about Titus County Cares, visit their website: www .tituscountycares.org.
2. Fay Hanleybrown, John Kania, and Mark Kramer, "Channeling Change: Making Collective Impact Work," *Stanford Social Innovation Review*, 2012. For further information, visit www.ssireview.org.
3. Ibid.
4. For more information about the Cy-Hope Centers, visit their website: www.cy-hope.org.

DISCUSSION GUIDE

THIS DISCUSSION GUIDE IS designed for a group study of *Kingdom Come*. The questions are arranged by chapter so that you can adjust for a shorter or longer study, as best fits your needs. Feel free to focus on the questions or issues that resonate most with your group; the guide is intended as a basis for deeper conversation, community, and spiritual growth, so use it as a starting point and let God guide your time together.

INTRODUCTION

1. What is your definition of the word *church*?

   Little c vs. Big C (building vs. people)

2. What does it mean to partner with God in his redemptive mission in the world?

3. What is your understanding of *the Kingdom of God*? How is *the Kingdom* the same as or different from the church? *Inbreaking Already not yet.*

   Present but incomplete.

4. Explain why you agree or disagree with the following statements:

   a) God's primary agenda on earth focuses on building the church.

   b) What happens on Sunday mornings largely defines the mission and ministry of the church.

   c) If people aren't going to church on Sunday, then something is terribly messed up with the pursuit of God's agenda.

5. What would it look like and what would happen if the Kingdom of God became *visible* and *active* in our daily experience here on earth?

1: MY JOURNEY INTO THE KINGDOM

1. How would you define the church's mission in the world?

   Build up to send out

2. Jesus told us to pray, "Thy *Kingdom* come," not "Thy *church* come." How does this statement affect how we should view what we do?

3. What do you think Jesus meant when he said, "I have come to give you abundant life"? What does it mean to live abundantly?

4. Reggie says, "Kingdom engagement thrusts us into situations where abundant life is threatened,

compromised, or missing, so that we can serve as advocates for the life that God intends for people to experience." What situations are you aware of in your neighborhood, town, or area? How can you serve as an "advocate for life" there? *Homeless*

5. How has the church's engagement with the surrounding culture changed during your lifetime? What is the church's role in the culture?

2: KINGDOM TALES

1. How is God's Kingdom similar to earthly kingdoms? How do they differ?

2. In Matthew 13:24-47, Jesus compares the Kingdom of Heaven to a farmer who planted good seed; a mustard seed planted in a field; the yeast that a woman used in making bread; the treasure that a man discovered hidden in a field; a merchant on the lookout for choice pearls; and a fishing net that was thrown into the water and caught fish "of every kind." Which of these analogies do you most connect with? How can we apply it to our Kingdom living today? *The farmer + the seed. Don't worry about the soil, scatter everywhere!*

3. How did Jesus turn upside-down the prevailing notion about who will be favored in God's Kingdom? How does this understanding change or establish our perspective on the Kingdom?

4. How did Jesus *invade* the kingdom of Satan? How can we continue this invasion today?

3: THE HEROIC KINGDOM NARRATIVE

1. Reggie says, "When we were born, [we] were cast headlong into the story of the Kingdom. We didn't ask for the roles we were given or beg to be here. But here we are." What opportunities do you have to serve the Kingdom because of who you are, where you live, and the circumstances of your life?

2. What does it mean that "the Kingdom of God is primarily a mission, not just a message"?

3. Do you agree or disagree that "all efforts that enhance life as God intends are Kingdom efforts," even if they are "nonchurch" activities? Explain or discuss.

4. If it's true that advancing the Kingdom is God's primary activity on earth, how does this change your priorities, attitudes, and actions?

5. Describe a situation that you've experienced, witnessed, or heard about in which God flipped a strategy of the devil into an advance for the Kingdom of Heaven.

6. How does understanding that the Kingdom agenda belongs to the King, not to us, affect what we do and say?

4: CHALLENGING THE CHURCH'S STORYLINE

1. If we understand the Kingdom agenda as "creating opportunities for abundant life to break out in our communities," as Reggie asserts, how do you feel about including Hindus, Muslims, Buddhists, or others in the Kingdom agenda?

2. What are some signs of church-centeredness that you've observed in your congregation? What are some signs of Kingdom-centeredness that you've observed in your congregation? What is the fundamental difference between the two?

3. Whether you are a leader or part of the flock, how can you promote a more Kingdom-centered perspective in your congregation or small group? What needs to change?

4. In a Kingdom-centered perspective, how do we measure progress or success? How does this differ from a church-centered perspective?

5. How does viewing ourselves as *pilgrims* or *exiles* change our understanding of the Kingdom and our perspective on our mission in life?

5: AIDING AND ABETTING THE KINGDOM

1. How does a Kingdom-centered narrative affect how we "do church"? How does it affect *where* and *how*

we worship, and *who* is authorized to do *what* in our church gatherings?

2. What is the role of the Holy Spirit in fulfilling the Kingdom narrative? In what ways have we hindered or complicated the work of the Spirit?

3. What does it mean that God's people are "a kingdom of priests"? How does viewing yourself as a priest affect how you engage with and participate in the mission of God?

4. How does viewing ourselves as priests affect the *content* of our gatherings as the church? How does it affect our *programming*?

5. How does a Kingdom-centered perspective affect our concept of discipleship? What changes in what we do, as leaders and as members of the congregation, might be in order?

6. Describe your understanding of *calling* (vocation). How does a Kingdom-centered perspective change how you see your vocation?

6: WHEN IT WORKS: KINGDOM COLLABORATION

1. Using the story of Titus County Cares as an example, describe a situation you've seen in which Kingdom collaboration has produced positive results.

2. What are some opportunities in your community for cross-domain collaboration?

3. How might your congregation become a champion of and financial provider for a cross-domain collaboration?

4. In this chapter, Reggie identifies nine obstacles to pursuing a Kingdom-centered agenda. Which of these are you most likely to face in your particular situation? What can you do to overcome these obstacles?

5. What is one change you can make in your congregation as a result of reading this chapter?

7: MAKING THE MOVE

1. Do you feel anxious or reluctant about moving toward a Kingdom-centered ministry? What specifically is holding you back?

2. What changes can you make to move from leading an *institution* to leading a *movement*?

3. What do you currently *celebrate*, *reward*, or *value* in the life of your congregation? How can you celebrate, reward, or value Kingdom-centered activities?

4. Do you anticipate any hesitation or resistance from other people as you seek to change the scorecard for your congregation? What are some ways you can

address their concerns while still working together toward a common goal?

5. In the chapter, Reggie discusses ten tips for preparing to lead a movement. Which ones do you find the most helpful? Which ones do you need to focus on to get a movement started?

8: WHAT NOW?

1. Based on the suggestions in this chapter, create an action plan for moving toward a Kingdom-centered ministry. If you're reading this book as part of a group, share your plan with the group.

2. What is a small, sure-win project you can start with?

3. What breaks your heart, or what are you most passionate about?

4. What changes can you make in your prayer life as you strive for a Kingdom-centered church?

5. What are some strengths you bring to the table? What are some areas in which you could improve as you start this movement?

CONCLUSION

1. How has your perspective on the church and the Kingdom of God changed because of reading this book?

2. How has this book given you hope?

3. How has this book given you a sense of urgency in pursuing "thy Kingdom come"?

ABOUT THE AUTHOR

DR. REGGIE McNEAL has helped to shape the church leadership conversation through his extensive speaking schedule and work as an author. He enjoys helping people, leaders, and Christian organizations determine and experience epic wins in their pursuit of greater intentionality and impact. He serves as the missional leadership specialist for Leadership Network of Dallas, Texas.

Currently, Reggie is working with community leaders around the country to build cross-domain collaborative efforts that can move the needle on big societal issues. In addition, he provides coaching and consultation for individuals and teams in becoming more missionally focused and Kingdom biased in their ministry approaches.

Reggie served in local church leadership for more than twenty years, including as founding pastor of a new congregation. His past experience includes time as a denominational executive and as a leadership development coach. Reggie has lectured or taught as adjunct faculty for multiple seminaries, including Fuller, Southwestern Baptist, Golden Gate Baptist,

Trinity Evangelical Divinity School, Columbia International, and Seminary of the Southwest. He has also resourced the United States Army Chief of Chaplains Office, the Chaplains Training School at Fort Jackson, Air Force chaplains, and the Air Force Education and Training Command.

Reggie's work also extends to the business sector, including the Gallup Organization, in addition to his role as an advisory board member for several ministry organizations.

Reggie's education includes a BA degree from the University of South Carolina, and MDiv and PhD degrees from Southwestern Baptist Theological Seminary.

Reggie and his wife, Cathy, make their home in Columbia, South Carolina.

ALSO BY REGGIE MCNEAL

Get Off Your Donkey! Help Somebody and Help Yourself

*A Work of Heart: Understanding How God Shapes
Spiritual Leaders*

*Missional Communities: The Rise of the Post-
Congregational Church*

The Present Future: Six Tough Questions for the Church

*Missional Renaissance: Changing the Scorecard for
the Church*

*Revolution in Leadership: Training Apostles for
Tomorrow's Church*

*Practicing Greatness: Seven Disciplines of Extraordinary
Spiritual Leaders*

Get a Life! It Is All about You

*Rediscover the five gifts
that launched an unstoppable*

MOVEMENT OF GOD.

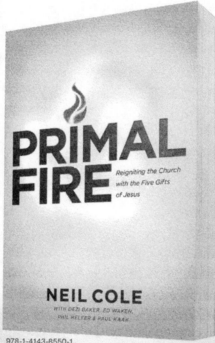

978-1-4143-8550-1

Learn the surprising truth about the five gifts of Jesus—
what they mean, how they reflect Christ, and the remarkable
power and synergy that result when we all work to
ignite the church's full potential and passion.

It's time to become the gifts that Christ intended for us to be.

CP0911

PLEASING GOD DOESN'T HAVE TO BE SUCH HARD WORK.

THE WELL-PLAYED LIFE

WHY PLEASING GOD DOESN'T
HAVE TO BE SUCH HARD WORK

LEONARD SWEET

Bestselling author of *Jesus Manifesto*
and *The Gospel According to Starbucks*

978-1-4143-7362-1

Do you secretly think that the harder you work, the more God is pleased with you? Join renowned author Len Sweet on a journey toward experiencing the fullness of joy that comes from enjoying (and being enjoyed by) God. Knowing how to play well—in every stage of our lives—is the key to turning a life of work into a life filled with God-pleasing richness.

CP0912

BECOME THE
GOOD NEWS PEOPLE
THAT WE WERE MEANT TO BE.

978-1-4143-9015-4

When you hear the word *evangelical*, do you think *good news*? That's what the word means, but too often that's not how others see evangelical Christians. In *Revangelical*, learn how we can realign our hearts with the things that most concerned Jesus and discover what it means to live as Good News people. The revangelical movement is changing the world—are you ready to join it?

CP0913